The Wines of Texas

Other books by Sarah Jane English
(published by Eakin Press):

Top Chefs in New Orleans
Top Chefs in Texas
Vin Vignettes: Stories of Famous French Wines

The Wines of Texas

A Guide and a History

Sarah Jane English

EAKIN PRESS ★ Austin, Texas

THIRD EDITION
1995

Revised Edition — 1989
Copyright © 1986
By Sarah Jane English
Published in the United States of America
By Eakin Press
A Division of Sunbelt Media, Inc.
P.O. Drawer 90159 ★ Austin, Texas 78709

ISBN 1-57168-054-3

5   6   7   8   9   10

Library of Congress Cataloging-in-Publication Data

English, Sarah Jane
    The Wines of Texas, A Guide and a History.

    Includes index.
    1. Wine and wine making — Texas. I. Title.
TP557.E54   1995   641.2'2'09764   86-11434
ISBN 1-57168-054-3

To my favorite Wilsons – two precious friends:

Barbara Elaine Wilson Fuller
Ruth Elinor Wilson Melton

About the Author

How long, how long,
In infinite pursuit
Of this and that endeavor and dispute?
Better be merry with the fruitful grape
Than sadden after none, or bitter, fruit.
                        — The Rubaiyat of Omar Khayyam

Sarah Jane English is the author of four books on food and wine: *Vin Vignettes: Stories of Famous French Wines; The Wines of Texas, A Guide and a History; Top Chefs in Texas;* and *Top Chefs in New Orleans.*

She is a free-lance writer, a spokesman for the American wine industry, and a noted connoisseur of wines. English is considered the foremost wine writer in the Southwest, concentrating on California, Texas, and French wines. Her book on Texas wines was introduced by a resolution to the United States Congress as the definitive authority on the subject and was so recorded in the *Congressional Record.*

English has conducted seminars for Foods and Wines from France, the official promotional agency for the French government, and works with them on special projects. She is a wine consultant and presents programs for professional, civic, social and charitable organizations and conducts wine tastings for various groups. She travels to California several times a year and to France annually to taste wines and to keep up to date on the markets.

The author appears on television and radio talk shows in several states to speak about the wine industry as well as food and travel and is a featured speaker at conventions and events around the country. She teaches a wine course in her home and designs and escorts tours to France, California, and other wine regions for AAA travel agency. The author has taken the intensive course "Fundamentals of Table Wine Processing" at the University of California at Davis, the one-week course on German wines given by H. Sichel Sohne, Inc., in Germany, the Sterling Viticultural Seminar, Seagram Classic School of Service and Hospitality, Cakebread American Harvest Workshop, as well as numerous other seminars on wine, such as World Vinifera Conference in Seattle, Washington, and Vinexpo in Bordeaux, France. She is a popular speaker and in demand for her programs, which include *The Art of Tasting Wine, California Varietals, Wines From Start to Finish, History of Texas Wines, Pairing Wine and Food,* and *The Process of Making Wine.*

She is active in various wine and food organizations: International Who's Who in Wine; Ordre des Coteaux de Champagne; Confrerie des Chevaliers du Tastevin; a former officer in the Confrerie de la Chaine des Rotisseurs; Society of Wine Educators; American Institute of Wine and Food; a founding board member of the Texas Hill Country Wine & Food Festival; the first wine-writer recipient of "Who's Who in Food and Wine" in Texas (April 1988), and Les Dames d'Escoffier.

A native of Dallas, the author is a fifth-generation member of an historic Texas family which includes James English — her great, great-grandfather and the first circuit-riding Methodist minister in Texas. Her father, Clarence English, was a pioneer in the transportation industry in the Lone Star state and one of the first Texans to pilot his private plane for business purposes. English attended Hockaday School and Highland Park High School before obtaining her B.A. and M.A. degrees from the University of Texas at Austin. The author makes her home at 2107 Hartford Road, Austin, Texas 78703.

Contents

Foreword

And wine can of the wise their wits beguile,
Make the sage frolic, and the serious smile.
— Homer

The story of winegrowing in Texas is one of the most dramatic in the entire history of winegrowing in America. From a single tiny old-fashioned wine cellar and thirty acres of vines in 1974, viniculture in Texas exploded in a little over a decade to thousands of acres and twenty-seven wineries, some of them already producing wines that are winning medals in competition with the finest wines in the world. To fully express the fascinating quality of this story would require an opera or at least an epic motion picture.

In *The Wines of Texas, A Guide and a History*, Sarah Jane English captures in colorful detail the stories of the modern winegrowers who are making vinicultural history in the Lone Star state. While her book echoes the loyalty that might be expected of a fifth-generation Texan, it accurately describes in personal interviews the beginnings and the progress of the state's winegrowing pioneers.

It also provides guidance for touring the wineries, a sample pairing of Texas wines and foods, ideas on tasting wines and entertaining, and recipes from the winegrowers' wives.

— LEON ADAMS

Preface

Wine measurabley drunk and in season
Bringeth gladness to the heart
And cheerfulness to the mind.
— Ecclesiastes

In June 1986, at the San Francisco Fair and Wine Competition, two Texas wineries took top honors: the Llano Estacado 1984 Chardonnay, Slaughter-Leftwich Vineyards, won a double gold medal, and the Pheasant Ridge 1983 Cabernet Sauvignon won a gold medal. This nationally prestigious competition, open to all American wines, features the most respected wine judges in the business. All wines are tasted blind — without knowing names or geographical locations. Of the 1,955 wines entered, eleven were awarded double gold medals, and 54 wines won gold medals. Older vines, of course, make better wine, which only sweetens the victory for the Texas wines. The Cabernet Sauvignon at Pheasant Ridge was planted in 1979 — young by any standards — and the Llano Estacado Chardonnay vines are about the same age. Clearly, this was an outstanding performance by two Texas wineries. And that was only the beginning.

After an incredibly brief period of time, Texas is growing world-class wines. It began in the early 1970s, when test plots for vineyards were planted by modern pioneers such as Clint McPherson, Ed Auler, and Bobby Smith. They envisioned a commercial wine industry for Texas and did the groundwork to make that dream a reality.

Part of the reality was understanding Texas laws that have restricted winegrowing since the Prohibition era. In the Lone Star state, more than half the 254 counties were dry. Texas law did not permit wine production in dry counties, and since much of the best soil for wine grapes is in those counties, the law was a real threat to the industry. It took legislative action initiated by Ed Auler and Bobby Smith for wine production to occur in dry areas. Auler and Smith accomplished that legislation in 1978. Still, selling wine to the public is not permitted in some of the dry areas, although it may be sold to wholesalers and retailers. Consequently, people who visit the wineries can taste the wine, but they can't buy it on the premises. Wineries located in wet counties, where wines may be sold on the property, have a competitive edge. Some wineries located in dry counties have managed the additional expense of purchasing land in wet counties and constructing a separate tasting facility.

Several disadvantages apply to all wineries. They are prohibited from providing promotional wine for any occasion, including wine competitions. Organizations or judging committees have the expense of buying wines from retailers or wholesalers rather than having it donated. The rule discourages competitions and ultimately denies awards which help inform the public about products. It is also against the law for vintners to give their wine to charity events, fund-raisers, or to writers for review. Nor can they give their wine to restaurateurs who understandably must taste a wine before including it on a wine list. Auler has originated a new association, the Winery Council, composed of estate vintners to help solve some of the ongoing problems of the industry.

After a great amount of research and trial and error, Llano Estacado Winery was bonded for winemaking in 1976, La Buena Vida Vineyards in 1978, and Fall Creek Vineyards in 1979. Most of the other wineries in Texas weren't bonded until the 1980s, including Texas-size Ste. Genevieve, an addition of paramount importance to the Texas wine industry. In a short period, Texas grape growers and winemakers have managed to produce some of the finest vinous beverages in America. They have planted *Vitis vinifera* (European wine grapes, not native American stock) where they had been told it wouldn't grow, and the stock is producing wine grapes that are fine enough to compete with older and more established vines from the best regions of California, or anywhere else in the world.

Texas' microclimates permit a variety of wine grapes to thrive in various soils. Drip irrigation, soil analysis, proper location, wind currents, and other climatic conditions permit vineyards to exist where it had been thought to be impossible. Like most things worthwhile, grapes need tender loving care. Texas grape growers and vineyard managers understand these necessities and are providing them. After all, wine begins in the vineyard. The best wine is made from the best grapes.

State-of-the-art technology is taking a lot of the guesswork out of making wine as well as adding other significant contributions. Texas vintners are dedicated. They expect the finest quality from their considerable investments and are not willing to settle for less than the best.

Representatives of the wine industry, whether growers, winemakers or owners, have done their homework. Their combined knowledge and efforts are working to win a place for Texas wines among the most distinguished in the world.

Long ago France established the superb hallmark for fine winemaking, and the worldwide respect for French wines is without precedent. In 1976, American wines competed with French wines in a blind tasting held in Paris and judged by Frenchmen. California wines, including Chateau Montelena Chardonnay and Stag's Leap Wine Cellars Cabernet Sauvignon, outscored *grand crus* French wines, a feat that was a turning point for establishing the acceptance of the American wine industry.

In 1991, Dr. George Ray McEachern, an extension horticulturist at Texas A&M University, organized a similar event called the "Texas/France Shoot-Out" held at the Texas Department of Agriculture in Austin. The twelve judges included two Frenchmen. Eight Texas Chardonnays, ranging in price from $8.99 to $15.49, successfully competed against four French burgundies, costing from $20 to $65 a bottle.

The 1989 Messina Hof Texas Chardonnay Private Reserve won first place. The tie for second place went to the 1990 Fall Creek Chardonnay Texas Grand Cuvée and 1989 Llano Estacado Texas Chardonnay. The French wines were 1989 Macon-Lugny Les Genievres, 1987 Puligny-Montrachet Premier Cru Les Gareness Chartron et Trebuchet, 1986 Corton-Charlemagne Pierre Andre Grand Cru, and 1987 Laroche Chablis Premier Cru.

McEachern remarked, "This contest symbolizes a coming of age for Texas wines."

And the good times continue.

In 1994, Messina Hof "Angel" Late Harvest Johannisberg Riesling was the first Texas wine in ten harvests to earn a double gold medal, this time at the Tasters Guild International Wine Judging in Fort Lauderdale, Florida. And *The Wine Spectator* magazine gave "Angel" a 90 in 1992, ranking it the best regional wine.

The 1993 Slaughter-Leftwich Vineyards Sauvignon Blanc won a gold medal in the 10th Annual *Dallas Morning News* National Wine Competition, considered one of the top competitions in the country. Hill Country Cellars won a silver medal for its 1992 Merlot, and Fall Creek won a silver for its 1992 Semillon-Sauvignon Blanc. Judges tasted more than 1,400 wines from twenty-one states.

By 1995, many Texans had developed very sophisticated palates and they expected the good wines that Texas is capable of producing. Texas' excellent white wines, and especially the Chardonnays, had garnered many national and international awards. There were a number of good red wines as well: Llano Estacado Signature Red, Fall Creek Granite Red Reserve, Llano Estacado Cabernet Sauvignon, Grape Creek Cabernet Trois, Cap✦Rock Cabernet Sauvignon, Messina Hof Cabernet Sauvignon and its Traditions series, Ste. Genevieve Proprietor's Reserve Cabernet Sauvignon, Cap✦Rock Cabernet Royale, and Pheasant Ridge Reserve Cabernet Sauvignon.

Zelma Long, president of Simi Winery in California, remarked at the 1995 Texas Hill Country Wine and Food Festival, "I think it is really important for Texans to support their wine industry. When I was here seven years ago, I noticed the pioneering efforts and I still admire that Texan quality. We have so many resources in California, but you're really still doing major pioneering efforts here." And at the same festival, after Charlie Wagner of Caymus tasted the Messina Hof Reserve Cabernet Sauvignon, he said, "I must say, I was impressed by the Messina Hof Cabernet. It is commendable and much better than I had anticipated."

Paul Bonarrigo's double-barrel approach to winemaking at Messina Hof must be working. He puts red wine in one new American oak barrel for a year and then moves it to another new American barrel for more aging. Additionally, he believes that the Chardonnay grape really lends itself to the process. According to him, the difference between a good Texas Chardonnay and a French Montrachet is about $60.

Fall Creek owner Ed Auler thinks the quality of Texas wines is higher than it has ever been and that it will continue to get even better. He believes the vines just need more age.

Ste. Genevieve winemaker Don Brady says the reason Ste. Genevieve is sold mostly in Texas is because their wine sales here are growing so rapidly they don't need to go out of state. Also, it's extremely expensive to sell outside the state.

Bill Stephens, wine writer for the *San Antonio Express*, said, "Texas Chardonnays are for real — they're not just an anomaly anymore. The Texas wine industry is valid."

The future of Texas wines is certain, as an industry which has piqued the interest of farmers, ranchers, landowners, and those looking for second careers. Delicious wines will certainly be produced for a public with an increasing curiosity, knowledge, and desire for the best.

It has been said that when one drinks the fine Texas wines, it makes one believe there really is a Bacchus.

— S. J. E.

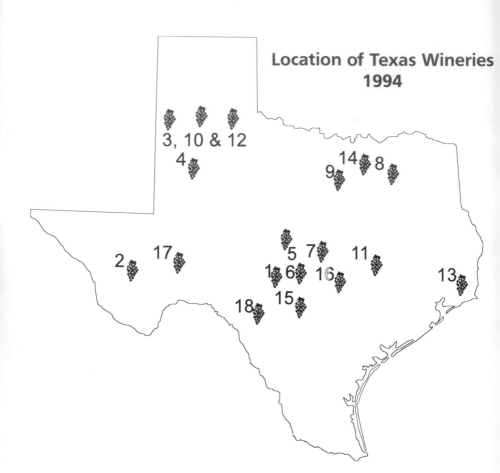

Location of Texas Wineries 1994

3, 10 & 12
4
14 8
9
2 17
5 7 11
1 6 16
13
18 15

1 Bell Mountain Winery (Fredericksburg)
2 Blue Mountain Vineyard (Fort Davis)
3 Cap✛Rock Winery (Lubbock)
4 Delaney Vineyards, Inc. (Lamesa)
5 Fall Creek Vineyards (Tow)
6 Grape Creek Vineyards (Stonewall)
7 Hill Country Cellars (Cedar Park)
8 Homestead Winery (Ivanhoe)
9 La Buena Vida Vineyards (Springtown)

10 Llano Estacado Winery (Lubbock)
11 Messina Hof Wine Cellars (Bryan)
12 Pheasant Ridge Winery (Lubbock)
13 Piney Woods Country Wines (Orange)
14 Preston Trail Winery (Gunter)
15 Sister Creek Vineyards (Sisterdale)
16 Slaughter Leftwich Vineyards (Austin)
17 Ste. Genevieve Wines (Ft. Stockton)
18 Val Verde Winery (Del Rio)

Source: Texas Wine Marketing Research Institute, Texas Tech University; and Texas Alcoholic Beverage Commission

Acknowledgments

I often wonder what the vintners buy
One half so precious as the goods they sell.
 — The Rubaiyat of Omar Khayyam

Writing a book on wines is a joyous endeavor. People in the wine industry are among the most gracious, hospitable, dedicated, and charming members on the planet. They, and so many others, made this book a reality; for instance, Leon Adams and Marvin Overton, whose encouragement and support have been tremendously important to me. And, of course, I am deeply grateful for the time and interest of so many incredible Texans.

Thank you Nancy Hamilton for being such a great resource and giving me so many meaningful references. Thank you Pid Wilson Melton for clipping newspapers weekly and sending me all the wine articles. Thank you Barbara Wilson Fuller for reading, proofing, and discussing the book; you too, Mollie Hawkins Sharpe, Liz Carpenter, and Martha Coons. Thank you Susan and Ed Auler for your resources and information, and for housing the second manuscript. Thank you George Ray McEachern for driving to Austin to interview and record the modern history of the Texas wine industry. Thank you Millie Howie for wanting to publish the stories of Texas wines. Thank you Larry Peel for all the subscriptions and advice. Thank you Danny Presnal for always answering my telephone calls and questions. Thank you Charles McKinney for the information on the University of Texas wine project. Thank you Roy Renfro for the overview on the T. V. Munson Center. Thanks to Tim

Dodd, for his invaluable statistical organization of the modern Texas wine industry. Thanks also to the supportive Texas agriculture commissioner, Rick Perry, and to Jeff Phillips for his tireless efforts in promoting *The Wines of Texas*. Thanks to Nanci Haehnel and Jeff Farrell of Haehnel Farrell Associates for book cover suggestions, including the one used. Thanks to OMNI Austin Hotel General Manager Thomas Schurr for sponsoring the annual inauguration of Texas Wine Month (October) at the OMNI Austin, for featuring the first and only all Texas wine menu in Austin at ancho's restaurant, and for showcasing *The Wines of Texas*. And many thanks to all the cooperative Texas vintners, winemakers, their wives, and staff members for time, interviews, photographs, and so much more.

Introduction

Thou hast made us to drink the wine of astonishment.
— Psalms 60:3

During the past twenty years the world has undergone a wine revolution. Countries with little or no history in producing quality wines are now competing with traditional winemaking regions such as France and Italy. Countries such as New Zealand, Australia, and Chile have not only captured the major share of their own wine markets but are now substantial exporters as well. This wine revolution has also influenced the culture of many of these countries. Wine, which was once perceived as primarily a beverage for the elite, is becoming a more integral part of ordinary people's lives.

The Texas wine industry has also experienced significant growth during the past two decades, and change continues at a rapid pace. Some wineries have been forced to close, while others have consolidated their position and appear stronger than ever.

Texas wines continue to receive recognition from around the world. From 1990 to 1993, for example, thirty-one gold medals were awarded to Texas wines at national and international wine competitions. As the demand for quality Texas wines has grown, Texas wineries have expanded their share of the local market from 2% in 1991 to nearly 6% in 1994. Texans are notoriously proud of their state, and this pride is increasingly reflected in their purchasing loyalty toward local wines.

The Texas wine industry also has an important economic impact. Each year the industry has a direct and indirect impact of more than $100 million on the Texas economy, employs more than 2,000 people, and contributes greater than $5 million in taxes to the state treasury. As the industry continues to develop, the impact on the economy of Texas will also grow.

One of the most recent developments has been the success of new festivals and wine-related events. For example, the city of Grapevine (between Dallas and Fort Worth) has committed to developing the Texas wine industry, and their annual wine and food festivals (such as Grapefest, and the Texas New Vintage Festival) now attract more than 100,000 visitors each year. The Texas Hill Country Wine and Food Festival has also become a major event that helps to educate consumers regarding Texas wines. In other regions throughout the state (from Lubbock, San Angelo, Houston, and Bryan/College Station), events are being organized that combine Texas wines and food and attract thousands of consumers.

Although the future of the Texas wine industry appears bright, many viticultural, enological, and marketing challenges must be overcome if industry expansion is to continue. Nonetheless, opportunities exist for people who are committed to long-term involvement and who have the resources and abilities to take up the challenges. Grape growers, winery owners, distributors, retailers, educators, promoters, political representatives, and others have all played a role in helping the industry reach its current position. These individuals and groups need to continue to work together if they wish to sustain this growth.

The previous editions of *The Wines of Texas* have been well received by people from a variety of backgrounds. This edition is a timely update, as many exciting developments have occurred throughout Texas since the last edition was published in 1989. New personalities have become involved, and others who were part of the original revolution continue to play critical roles. Sarah Jane English provides a fascinating overview of some of the important personalities and events in this dynamic industry.

— TIM H. DODD, PH.D.

1

Tracing the Vines to Earlier Times

Therefore God gave thee of the dew of heaven, and the fatness of the earth, and plenty of corn and wine.
— Genesis 27:28

Rugged, six-foot-tall Texans didn't come with the land. Neither did the exceptional Texas ladies who graced the state. There were no natives. The individualists who stamped human dignity with a special Texas brand have evolved, and, like the history they created, are an integral part of the land that tells their story. The men and women who tamed the Lone Star state were special: They had to be. Its earth didn't yield bounty willingly and demanded the most from anyone trying to take it. It still does.

The first people on the future soil of Texas were invaders, Siberian hunters who trekked across the land mass connecting Asia and Alaska about 12,000 years ago. They ate their way down to the High Plains of Texas and can be found there today representing the oldest remains of man in the New World, a dubious distinction. Anyway, the weather changed over thousands of years and the land and animals changed with it. There was less water and more sun. The land accommodated the weather, and man accommodated the land or became extinct.

Relics and bones of the primitives have been discovered on property owned by the University of Texas System, land turned into vineyards that are producing wine for

1

Ste. Genevieve near Fort Stockton. Wine from the land of Texas — and it's good, very good.

The primitives, however, did not drink wine. Actually, they were more meat than potato men, even though they seldom lived long enough to cultivate the land had they thought of it. They usually died before they were nineteen years old, and it must hardly have seemed worth the effort. Besides, the folks were small, and a rather large group of them could live quite comfortably for some time off one of the giant bison — some with a six-foot horn spread — or mastodons then available on the waving grasslands of the Texas High Plains. These hunters were eager eaters and unfortunately had soon devastated the game. Afterwards, the primitives moved south.

The next peoples on the Texas scene were the American Indians. They came from Asia too, and like their predecessors, did not drink wine. However, one group of them is credited with inventing firewater. "The Coahuiltecans dissolved ground red Texas laurel beans in mescal to produce firewater," historian T. R. Fehrenbach wrote. Considering their ghastly diet — which included worms, insects, rotting wood, and deer dung — the heftier beverage was essential. These Coahuiltecans lived around Del Rio and along the Rio Grande, home area of the Val Verde Winery, the oldest winery in Texas still producing. It was established in 1883.

Among the oldest Indian tribes in Texas were the Tonkawas. They liked the Edwards Plateau and the Texas Hill Country, particularly for hunting deer, fishing, collecting the native pecans, and gathering berries from the wild grapevines. There are many Indian burial mounds on the Hill Country ranch surrounding Fall Creek Vineyards, and they have been preserved by owners Susan and Ed Auler.

Tonkawas didn't make wine either. They hunted bison on foot. After the Siberian hunters ate all the native horses, Indians had to wait until the sixteenth century for horse transportation. That's when the Spanish reintroduced the animal to America. Hunting bison on foot was no picnic, even though Tonkawa bows and arrows were a slight improvement over earlier man's rock and spear. The pre-horse culture was tough. Tonkawas called themselves "the most human of men," perhaps because they were less inclined toward cannibalism than the coastal Karankawas. All modern Texas Indians, except the Comanches, were cannibals in varying degrees. It must have been much more convenient to whip up roast leg of neighboring tribesman than struggle in a fight with some enormous beast in order to eat dinner. And apparently man's flesh didn't stimulate the savage brain to concoct a Château Tonkawa 1528, the just right something to marry well with hominid prime rib. In any event, the Indians did not make wine from the prolific native vines. Of approximately twenty-six species of grapes in the world, represented by more than 2,000 varieties, Texas has more than half of them. By far the largest concentration is in the Texas Hill Country and the Edwards Plateau, an area that also contains many Texas wineries.

If there had been a candidate for winemaker among these early Texians, the Caddoan tribesmen would have won the honor without contest. They were agriculturists and lived in the lush, rich Piney Woods. They grew potatoes, beans, yams, corn, tomatoes, and squash — crops first planted in America and later introduced abroad. Unlike the fearsome Apache warriors, and eventually the unequaled Comanche horsemen, the Caddos had a hierarchical government system. They lived in villages and were for the most part homebodies. By far, they were the most agreeable tribes to explorers and settlers. When the Spanish arrived, the Caddoan tribe members greeted them with *teychas*, their word for "friends" or "allies." So that's what the Spanish called them, *Tejas* in Spanish, and often spelled "x" instead of the "j" — hence, Texas. They gave the name to the land, and wineries in the state have honored both versions.

The Spanish *did* drink wine. When they came to Texas seeking gold, they carried it with them, as well as grapevine cuttings and a knowledge of viticulture. Of course, the Spanish conquest of the New World brought Governor Francisco Vasquez de Coronado from Mexico to Texas to vanquish empires and fill the coffers of the Crown, not to settle the

land. With the Coronado expeditions of 1540-42 were Indians. They formed the enslaved portion of the retinue that
followed the golden-armored governor and his plumed soldiers with their crimson banners waving behind the cross.
Religious men accompanied the entourage, priests both
kind and unyielding who were determined to purge the hea-
thens of their pagan ways. But these early explorations for
gold were just that, not attempts to colonize, and the adven-
turous *conquistadores* crossed the vast plains areas many
times in search of riches. Some Spaniards remained, and
Llano Estacado Winery in Lubbock is a name that com-
memorates the Spanish trek. Other wineries near Lubbock
are Pheasant Ridge, named for the native pheasants, and
Cap Rock, named for a geological formation.

About 120 years after Coronado trekked across the
High Plains and Llano Estacado regions, the first perma-
nent Spanish settlement was established in the El Paso area.
In 1659, two priests, Father Garcia de San Francisco y
Zuniga and Father Juan de Salazar, brought ten Chris-
tianized Indian families from the area to the present site of
Ciudad Juárez. Mission Señora de Guadalupe was the result.
Father Garcia and his charges accepted cultivation as an integral part of their missionary work, especially if they were
to survive in the windswept, semiarid country. But the
Franciscans also had to feed the soul, so they planted grapevine cuttings brought from Spain to create vineyards that
could produce sacramental wines for their mass. They
struggled to sustain the crops and themselves, often appeal-
ing for help from the custodian of the province, Fray Alonzo
de Posadas. Between 1660 and 1664, he sent them "three
thousand beeves, four thousand head of sheep and goats,
two thousand bullocks, two hundred mares and horses,
ploughshares, laborers, carpenters, implements, and other
necessaries."

In 1680, an Indian revolt in New Mexico drove the re-
sidual Spaniards into El Paso del Norte. Their arrival demanded more food, and once again Fray Alonso de Posadas
came to the rescue. Eventually, the Spanish presence stimulated agricultural production, and by 1682 there were four

missions in the area. Corpus Christi de la Isleta (now Ysleta), 1682, was one of them and is the oldest permanent settlement in Texas.

There were droughts and struggles and crop failures, but the Spanish government denied requests to abandon El Paso. It was an essential transportation pass between Mexico and New Mexico and a buffer zone to thwart hostile Indians. Against the Spanish *conquistadores*, however — mounted on their imported mustangs, covered with armor, and wielding swords of Toledo steel — Indians on foot were easily subdued. Stolen horses would challenge all that shortly.

Necessity spurred industry. A dam was constructed on the Rio Grande in 1684, and irrigation became a reality. The methods and contributions of the Iberians enhanced the valley. The dam was crude — willow branches were woven into tubular baskets, filled with stones, and placed side by side. Dams often washed away during the flood season, but they were easily rebuilt. Ditches were used as irrigation channels, and by 1726 the district was fertile and productive. According to the late University of Texas professor and librarian Carlos E. Castaneda, "wheat, corn, beans and all kinds of vegetables, as well as vineyards which produced delicious grapes, thrived."

The grapes were called El Paso or Mission grapes. Castaneda said they were equal to those of Spain, and the excellent wines made from Mission grapes were praised by many writers to El Paso for 200 years. Endowed with rich and fertile soil, the El Paso valley was capable of growing almost any product, but the farmers of the 1700s concentrated on these grapes and fruits typical of Europe. Muscatel and wild grapevines were also grown in the valley. Lt. Zebulon M. Pike was on military assignment when he was caught trespassing. He was arrested and taken to Chihuahua via El Paso del Norte. As the first Anglo to travel through the pass, March 1806, he recorded the event in his diary and wrote "numerous vineyards from which were produced the finest wine ever drank [*sic*]."

The Spanish settlement at El Paso was unique during

the seventeenth century, and it wasn't until French interests
threatened Spain that the Spanish made real efforts to settle
Texas. Having established their crimson and gold standard,
they intended to preserve their sovereignty.

France's greatest explorer, René Robert Cavelier, Sieur
de La Salle, planted the second flag in Texas in 1685. He
established Fort St. Louis at Garcitas Creek near Lavaca
Bay, and even though the colony was short-lived, it was the
beginning of a line of New World-bound Frenchmen that
made the Texas connection. And as far as wine is con-
cerned, the French penchant for the vinous beverage is
legendary.

Whether those first Frenchmen in Texas were influen-
tial as oenologists is not documented, but it is a fact that the
Anglo-American colonists enjoyed wine. Wherever they
moved, many made homemade wines from the native wild
vines or brought wine with them. The Pilgrims used white
wine to simmer sturgeon. Thomas Jefferson liked ham laced
with white wine. Black chefs on the Mississippi poached cat-
fish in white wine and made wine sauces to embellish the
dish. The old Menger Hotel, opened in San Antonio during
the 1850s, was the first luxurious hostelry in Texas. Its
famous black bean soup with sausages, garlic, wine, and a
touch of tabasco is still served.

When Stephen F. Austin brought the first colonists to
Texas in 1821, more than half the vast land area had never
been explored. The *Texas Almanac* reports that the white
population was less than 7,000, and the only towns of any
size were San Antonio, Goliad, and Nacogdoches. The
Spanish commissioners at Natchitoches (French for Nacogdoches) confirmed Governor Martinez's authorization for
young Austin to survey the county and choose a site for his
colony. Fehrenbach records that there were only thirty-six
inhabitants in Nacogdoches at that time and a few squatters
on the Spanish territory who had built log cabins in the for-
est to claim title: the Ambersons, Cartwrights, Englishes,
and Bells.

Beyond the small settlements stretched a wilderness, an
unknown land traversed by hostile, man-eating Indians.

Stephen F. Austin traveled extensively, searching for the best land. He chose the rich river bottom land between the Colorado and Brazos rivers in the southern coastal plains, away from the most dangerous Indian country. In his papers he later wrote, "Nature seems to have intended Texas for a vineyard to supply America with wines."

The *Telegraph and Texas Register*, May 9, 1837, reported a message to Congress on May 5, 1837, by President of the Republic of Texas Sam Houston. He made remarks regarding the trade of the Republic:

> Her cotton, sugar, indigo, wines, peltries, live stock, and the precious minerals will become objects of mercantile activity. To establish such intercourse with nations friendly to us, as will induce them to seek our markets with their manufactures and commodities, and receive from us in exchange our productions, will become our imperative duty.

After the War for Texas Independence, the capital was established at Houston, a town with plans still on the drawing board in 1836. However, in 1839 the capital was moved to Waterloo and renamed Austin. There was considerable disagreement about the choice. It was far from the settled frontier and constantly under threat of attack by hostile Comanches who liked to camp at the nearby springs. The interior colonists weren't all that safe from the savages either. As a matter of fact, Austin organized the first "rangers companies," later called the Texas Rangers, in the 1820s to patrol the frontier border. Nonetheless, Austin, "the greatest colonial proprietor in North American history" according to Fehrenbach, agreed with then President of the Republic Mirabeau Lamar that the location would encourage settlement of the interior. They were right. In 1840, there were about 900 people in Austin while the total population of Texas was approximately 39,000. According to the *Texas Almanac of 1857*, in 1850 Texas had a "total population of 212,592, of which 154,034 were white and 58,558 colored. June first there were 7 paupers in Texas and 6 criminals imprisoned in county jails, the Penitentiary not being open at that time." The total population in 1860 was 604,215, including 182,000 slaves. Galveston had the largest population, nearing 5,000, and the only other towns of any significance — San Antonio, Houston, New Braunfels, and Marshall — were struggling to maintain 1,000 persons in each place.

But the settlers kept on coming, and they discovered the wild grapevines. Ottilie Fuchs Goeth was one member of a family of German emigrants who moved to Texas in 1845. After she married, she raised her family on a sheep ranch at Cypress Mills. She recorded her memories of those days in the Texas Hill Country in a book, *Memoirs of a Texas Pioneer Grandmother*. One passage recalled how the day began with cooking a hearty breakfast for the family of nine plus the hands, tending the baby, preparing the bucket lunches for the men who wouldn't return to the house for lunch, cleaning the dishes, washing clothes, and preparing the midday meal. She wrote:

> All too fast, the morning was gone . . . But clomp, clomp, we hear horses. A company of Rangers on the trail of Indians has arrived. Everyone jumped to action. The riders unsaddled, washed and took care of the horses. Quickly Carl [her husband] had a mutton ready for roasting. There were vegetables and fruits and with it all a glass or two of the fiery Texas wine.

Penny and Dale Bettis of the now defunct Cypress Valley Winery owned the Goeth ranch before his death in 1989.

There were other reports about Texas viticulture cropping up. A monthly publication edited by J. D. B. De Bow, *De Bow's Review and Industrial Resources, Statistics, etc.*, reported on the Texas scene of August 1853:

> [Travels] . . . reminded us that our new and rapidly progressing state of Texas was beginning to show its excellent adaptation to the cultivation of the grape. We speak from actual observation. We have many a time feasted on the most delicious grapes in our rambles through the hills and along the limpid streams of Texas. We know that there is not a finer country in the world for the cultivation of the grape — not even la belle France. We

see by a late number of the *Houston Telegraph* that wine of
the finest quality is now produced in that state. The editor of the *Telegraph* says: "We are indebted to Col. William E. Crump for several bottles of excellent wine manufactured from the native grape. He has succeeded in
making a white wine from the Mustang grape which we
consider far better than the best samples of Catawba wine
that we have received from Cincinnati. The red wine he
had made from the same grape is of an excellent quality
and resembles the best claret; he has also made wine from
the winter grape, which ripens late in autumn. This wine
has delicious flavor, is of a deep red color, and resembles
the red Rhenish [*sic*] wine. The experiments which this
enterprising gentleman has made in the cultivation of the
native grapes indicate that the wines of Texas will soon be
as much sought for by the amateurs as the best wines
manufactured from the Catawba, Scuppernong, or Isa-
bella grape. We are confident that the vine can be cultivated to a far greater advantage in the undulating region
of Texas than in any other part of the Union. The climate
and soil resemble those of the best wine growing sections
of Europe and Asia."

It's difficult to believe that France's government felt
threatened by the Texas wine industry. Nonetheless, the
French *chargé d'affaires* was a vociferous reader of all publi-
cations, and he may have found pause in President Houston's remarks to Congress on the trade of the Republic. As a
representative of France he took steps to protect his
country's imports. France, of course, was the first European
power to recognize the Republic of Texas. A treaty was
signed by the French monarchy on September 25, 1839, and
a diplomatic agent was sent to Texas. He was a dandy and
excessively hypochondriacal, but true blue to the French
cause. A. Dubois de Saligny, *chargé d'affaires*, established the
official residence as "the French Legation in Texas," a modest stone structure that soon emitted reams of his papers.
He maintained an incredible correspondence with the
French minister, especially considering that there was no
postal service between Austin and Houston in 1840. One
simply found a wagon going that way or sent a personal cou-

rier. In a piece of correspondence dated February 4, 1840, de Saligny reviews the Republic of Texas tariff policy and concludes it favors the United States.

> Other nations . . . were taxed very high in light of the many pronouncements of the Texian government in favor of absolutely free trade. And either from bad luck or ignorance of the Texian legislators, to whom, I repeat, no hostility to France may be attributed, the very highest duties were on articles most likely to be supplied by French commerce (silks, fashions, ready-to-wear, *fancy goods*, and jewelry). There was a duty of twenty-five cents per gallon on all our wines without distinction of quality except for champagne which was taxed two dollars each dozen bottles. . . . I have protested incessantly . . . and have the satisfaction of reporting that I was completely successful in my efforts . . . and all duties on French wines imported directly from France have been abolished.

Relations between Texas and France were good. And while the new Republic was an unknown quantity to most Frenchmen and remained so even after statehood, feelings about the land were positive. Once they learned of it, French settlers wanted to come to Texas. Discouraged by the times that followed the French Revolution, they hoped to construct a more perfect society. Philosophically, a socialist approach to a better economy seemed the solution.

Socialism in France began as a middle-class movement. Communism developed at the same time from the needs of the working class. They were different. In the simplest terms, socialism contained precepts deriving from the old city-state ideas of ancient Greece as well as the medieval pattern of universal religion and economics — a spirit of cooperative good. In Texas, the pragmatic theory of capitalism — private enterprise and individual initiative for profit — was already well established. It didn't seem likely that the two doctrines could easily exist side by side.

Nonetheless, Victor Prosper Considérant, a Utopian socialist disciple of Charles Fourier, founded the old French colony named "La Reunion," and it was destined for the Dallas/Fort Worth area in 1855. Unlike La Salle's doomed expedition composed of "30 gentlemen adventurers with nothing better to do, 100 men — the scum of French ports, and some girls seeking husbands," the Dallas-bound bunch contained college graduates and professional people: bankers, engineers, physicians, agriculturists, geologists, distillers, a tinsmith, a locksmith, tailor, musician, and barber; indeed, a respectable potpourri of early pioneers. The charter accounted for the number of professional men and skilled artisans, calling for $1 million to finance the company. Shares cost $5, $25, and $100 and were available only to the financially solvent. In addition, only those who were highly regarded in their communities were recruited. Considérant said the success of the colony depended on a "high type of citizenry," and he placed the settlement where "he saw what seemed to be a bit of France." Considérant scouted the United States in 1853 for a proper site, according to William J. Hammond and Margaret Hammond in *La Reunion, a French Settlement in Texas.* His reaction to Texas, recorded in the Hammonds' book, was almost poetic.

> I was expecting something wild and rude, coarse grasses and weeds of enormous height, etc. The landscape was classic and charming; its character surprised us beyond all expression. In all civilized and cultivated America, I have seen nothing so sweet, so bewitching, so ornate and complete as these solitudes by which we entered the high basin of the Red River.

According to authors Hammond, Considérant was astonished when he found a "superior richness" of the soil, wild oats, numerous tender grasses, large forests, and many prosperous, cultivated fields. They wrote:

> Even the land which the Americans rejected as poor, rocky, and of thin soil, which they refused to cultivate, was exactly what the French needed to grow their vines . . . . Grapevines grown on such soil were of "lower growth and much less run to wood and leaf, than the kind which overspreads the bottoms [quoting Considérant] . . . . The latter reaches forth on all sides its gigantic branches and climbs to the summit of the largest trees, balancing between them its clusters of black grapes."

Near Dallas, at the junction of the forks of the Trinity,
Considérant met M. Gouhenans, chief of the first Icarian
vanguard, who gathered these wild grapes and made wine
out of them, which he sold for a dollar a bottle.

Several winery owners in adjacent Parker County
agreed with the French and located in the area: Château
Montgolfier, Sanchez Creek, La Buena Vida. Of the three,
only La Buena Vida remains in 1995. The capital proposed
for the old French settlement suggested $8,000 for farming
and gardening implements, $5,000 for horses and wagons,
and $35,000 for building materials, vines, seed, etc.

Newspaper articles followed the progress of the colony.
In February 1855, the *Dallas Herald* reported a visit by several men connected with La Reunion. In an interview it was
learned that they hoped to establish three provisional settlements: "It is their design to make everything they use within
themselves . . . and is especially their intention to engage
largely in the cultivation of the grape and manufacture of
wines."

Unfortunately, the colony was not successful. An article
in *The Texas State Gazette* explained one source of discon-
tent. "We would rather see the State a howling desert than
witness the spreading waves of Socialism stretch itself over
the Christian Churches and the Slave Institution of Texas,"
it reported.

According to historians, La Reunion also failed for a
number of other reasons. Apparently, Considérant lacked
the necessary skills for leadership. Also, the financial affairs
were badly mismanaged, and the project never received the
support or the involvement of the Americans – who were
expected to join the colony. They didn't join, with rare exceptions. In one such unusual instance, two Texas carpenters, who knew nothing about Fourier's Utopian socialism,
brought their wives to live in the colony. The ladies knew
even less than their husbands about economic philosophies,
and what was more, they were freethinking types. These gals
wore bloomers.

The last reason given for failure was climate. Old settlers said the winter of 1856–57 was the coldest one they

could recall, "fifteen degrees above zero inside the cabins and fifteen below outside."

While the French vines were dying in cold Dallas County, the grapes elsewhere in Texas were flourishing. In 1853, W. W. W. Davis, a sojourner to El Paso, wrote remarks about his visit. He described the land as fertile, well irrigated, and productive of fine crops.

> The climate is delightful, . . . a region of perpetual spring and summer. . . . The grape in its variety grows in great abundance, and vineyards, from which delicious wines are made, are scattered all along down the valley. DeBow says, "The most important production of the valley is grapes, from which are annually manufactured not less than *200,000 gallons of perhaps the richest and best wines in the world* [his emphasis]. This wine is worth two dollars per gallon and constitutes the principal revenue of the city. The El Paso wines are superior in richness, and flavor, and pleasantness of taste to anything in the United States, and I doubt not that they are superior to the best wines ever produced in the Valley of the Rhine or on the sunny hills of France."

While Davis and DeBow surveyed the agricultural situation, Texas' most illustrious frontiersmen brought an end to the disastrous Indian raids. Among the many legends about Texans, none is truer, more heroic or romantic than that of the Texas Rangers. They were imposing men, not so much for size—although most of them were six feet tall or more—but for their manner. Rangers were loners, quiet men whose modesty and demeanor surprised acquaintances. The horse was their home, and being constantly in the saddle gave them a rough appearance—bearded, dust-covered and without the benefit of fresh clothes or a shower. Looks deceived. Far from crude, their numbers included well-educated men whose campfire conversations frequently mentioned quotes from the classics. Strong and silent, the contradictions were real because the Rangers were exquisite warriors. Never in the history of America has a group of men, taken together or singly, been defined as more courageous and daring or more brutal in a fight. They fought the Comanche, not much given to gentlemanly combat but considered North America's finest horsemen, and they did so in his territory, far outnumbered.

Jack Hays has been described as the consummate Ranger. San Antonians believed the handsome twenty-three-year-old surveyor from Tennessee to be "a gentleman of purest character." He was the model for every Ranger that followed him. The gun that eventually gave Captain Hays and all the Rangers the edge over the Indians was Colt's revolving six-shooter, invented in 1838. Armed with a pair of the pistols, a rifle, and a knife, the Ranger seemed invincible. Perhaps his greatest weapon, however, was his reputation. The name Ranger filled the Indian with loathsome fear.

Rangers didn't drink wine. When there was a choice, Captain Hays liked to drink buttermilk. But he and his band of frontiersmen tamed the West so vineyards could eventually be developed there for the pleasure of wine-drinking Texans.

It is interesting to note the presidential welcoming of Texas as a Republic — more than a minor struggle, by the way. T. R. Fehrenbach in *Lone Star* reported that "President Jackson requested the Texas agents to come to the White House for 'the pleasure of a glass of wine.'"

In the early days, the Texas wine industry didn't have everyone's most generous thoughts. There were other opinions, much less glowing than DeBow's. One such man was John Russell Bartlett. He published a personal narrative of his explorations during the 1850s. A great traveler of the West, he ventured all the way to California. His assessment of El Paso wines adds a different dimension.

> The grape is the most extensively cultivated of all fruits. It resembles the Hamburgh grape, though not quite as large, and is said to have been brought from Spain. There are both white and purple varieties. Large vineyards of this delicious fruit are seen within the town and the district adjacent to El Paso. The vine is never staked or trailed. It is trimmed close in the fall; and in the spring it throws out its shoots from the very stump, near which

hangs the fruit. Each vine is kept separate, and the earth around freed from weeds. Careful cultivators cover the vines during the winter with straw. With the first opening of spring, the fields are irrigated or rather inundated; for the water is suffered to flow over them, and there to remain until the ground is thoroughly saturated. This is generally all the water they get. In July, the grapes come to maturity, and last full three months. . . . In order to extract the juice, grapes are thrown into large vats, trodden by the naked feet of men; after which they are put into bags or sacks of raw ox-hide and pressed. The wine of El Paso enjoys a higher reputation in certain parts of the United States than it deserves. I have drank [*sic*] little that was above mediocrity; and it served me as it does most others who are not used to it, causing a severe headache. . . .

While the renowned viticulturist Thomas V. Munson hybridized and classified grape species in Denison (1876) and Frank Qualia developed vineyards in Del Rio (1883), the grape growers around El Paso were looking at more than 200 years of viticultural history. In 1885, the El Paso telephone directory contained this bit of information:

Nearly all the ground around Paso del Norte is in vines. . . . The grape is known as the Mission grape. . . . It is hardy and laughs at insect plagues. About 600 vines can be planted to the acre, and require no further care than to be irrigated four times a year and covered in winter. Each vine will produce nearly a gallon of wine which, when one year old, sells for $2.00 a gallon. The wine produced . . . resembles pure Port, but has a slight tart flavor, which renders it an agreeable beverage in the heat of the summer. With age the brandy . . . nearly approaches the finest French product and is completely free from the heavy oils which are so destructive to the human stomache [*sic*].

But the early history records a disorganized wine production. The El Paso area showed great promise, but it was isolated from other developing regions and posed problems with transportation and commerce. There was a problem with the Spanish too. They were not eager for their New

World property to produce competitive wines. And as Anglos became the dominant inhabitants, there were religious differences. Protestants celebrated communion with unfermented grape juice and held strong beliefs about the evil of any alcoholic beverage.

After the Spanish, there was a scattered and sporadic wine production throughout the state, even though whiskey was the chosen beverage of the frontier. There were early attempts by German, French, and Italian settlers to establish vineyards; however, they were too busy fighting Indians and trying to survive to give the vines the attention they needed. The Texas wine industry at this point was from native vines, which were hearty and abundant but did not make very good wine.

According to Anthony "Tony" Truchard, his ancestor and namesake, Father Anthony Marie Truchard, purchased approximately 500 acres of land in southeast Texas in 1887 to establish a vineyard and winery similar to those of the Loire Valley in his native France. He paid "3,000 in gold coins," apparently derived from real estate ventures in Galveston with another Truchard brother.

"My great uncle, Father Truchard, brought his brother (my grandfather, Jean Marie Truchard) to a place in Texas now called Mentz to run the operation," Tony said. "Together they built a state-of-the-art winery and planted vines imported from France. The winery operation, like most in the United States, did not survive Prohibition."

But the building they built did survive, and Tony Truchard plans one day to restore it.

In addition to other grapes planted in 1887, two major varieties were the Herbemont and Black Spanish. Truchard is uncertain how long the winery and vineyards flourished. The poor weather conditions — heat and humidity — and then Prohibition caused his ancestors to go into other farming endeavors.

The vision of the two French pioneers in Texas was not lost on Jean Marie's young grandson Tony, who grew up on the farm with the old vineyard. He studied chemical engineering and then medicine, ultimately becoming a medical doctor. He and his wife, Jo Anne, now own Truchard Vineyards in the Carneros of Napa, California, and make excellent wines.

Early Texas viticulturists were dedicated farmers, but they were not alone in their interest in the vine. According to the *Dictionary of American History*, grape growing and winemaking were among the settlers' earliest occupations. French viticulturists were part of the Virginia Company experiment in 1619 to grow grapes and make wine. It failed, just as the attempts to make wine by many farmers in other states also failed until the mid-1800s. Then an Ohioan made a success of the Catawba grape, making Ohio the leading wine state in 1859 with a 568,000-gallon production. In 1984, 125 years later, that amount was paled by the largest producing winery in the United States, E. & J. Gallo. They had a storage capacity of 330 million gallons at four plants, according to the July 1988 issue of *Wines & Vines*. That magazine also reported Seagram Wine Company as the second largest with 87.75 million; Robert Mondavi was nineteenth with 8.5 million; Sebastiani was twenty-fourth with 6 million; Louis M. Martini was thirty-ninth with 3 million; and Ste. Genevieve Vineyards of Texas was fifty-seventh with a 1.5 million-gallon storage capacity. American wineries numbered approximately 1,250 in 1988.

There was a lot of Texas wine history between 1885 and the present, but not as much as there might have been. Prohibition caused an immense gap. In any event, things picked up in the late 1860s when thousands of immigrants interested in grape culture arrived in Texas from Europe. They crossed the native grapes such as the Mustang with European varieties. Some had vines shipped from California. Some used the native grapes. There must have been some degree of success because a Galveston customhouse report for 1867–68 listed exported wines valued at $835 with the value per gallon estimated at approximately one dollar. By 1885, there were several large vineyards near Houston; the annual production was 2,000 gallons. Local option elections the first decade of the twentieth century, however, showed Texans' sentiments about Prohibition and destroyed the Texas wine industry.

Regardless of how unpromising things looked in the early 1900s, they looked worse in 1845. Texas was a struggling young Republic then with seemingly little to recommend it. The United States was not an active suitor in courting Texas for annexation. Of the two, it was the young Republic that wanted the Union. Not that the U.S. didn't see the sense of the acquisition; Texas blocked the way to the Pacific. But the advantages definitely favored Texas — which needed money, protection, an orderly system of government, and business and cultural influences. In 1845, the scattered inhabitants numbered about 124,000, mostly farmers of little means and planters. There was no industry in Texas, and anything one bought was imported. A stop at the general store for staples meant buying salt, sugar, flour, molasses, and whiskey — and not necessarily in that order. There were few pleasures and an altogether absence of comfort in the outposts. A sip from the jug could soothe life on the rugged frontier.

Saloons preceded churches in town planning by a good bit and were the hub of all significant activity — social and political especially. As far as is known, wine was not on the menu. Whiskey was king.

Nonetheless, there were prohibitionist rumblings in the early Republic. A national organization called the Sons of Temperance garnered 3,000 Texas members, including the support of Sam Houston. Various laws for and against the sale of liquor came and went. More and more temperance unions organized, and the issue became political. The Constitution of 1876 offered local option and created the fragmented and confusing system that exists in the state today. Prohibition was a strong campaign issue in 1887. In 1908, 1909, and 1911, Prohibition amendments by the Democratic Executive Committee were narrowly defeated. World War I brought focus to the issue again. Finally, Texas adopted the federal government's amendment in 1918. It lasted for seventeen years in Texas, until August 1935, and virtually destroyed the Texas wine industry as well as that of the United States.

Author and wine expert Leon Adams summed up the situation in his book *The Wines of America*:

> The once proud American wine industry, which before 1900 had exported its wines around the world and won prizes . . . was reborn in ruins. It was making the wrong kinds of wine from the wrong kinds of grapes for the wrong kind of consumer in a whiskey-drinking nation with guilt feelings about imbibing in general and a confused attitude toward wine in particular.

But those days are over. America has climbed ever higher toward the pinnacle of winemaking success. France, of course, has represented the essence of fine winemaking, and the worldwide respect for French wines is without precedent. However, in 1976, when American wines competed with French wines and were judged by Frenchmen in Paris, California wines outscored *grand crus* French wines — a feat that brought acceptance to the American wine industry.

In 1991, Dr. George Ray McEachern, an extension horticulturist at Texas A&M University, organized a similar event called the "Texas/France Shoot-Out" at the Texas Department of Agriculture. The twelve judges included two Frenchmen. Eight Texas Chardonnays, ranging in price from $8.99 to $15.49, successfully competed against four French burgundies, costing from $20 to $65 a bottle.

The 1989 Messina Hof Texas Chardonnay Private Reserve won first place. The tie for second place went to the 1990 Fall Creek Chardonnay Texas Grand Cuvee and 1989 Llano Estacado Texas Chardonnay.

McEachern remarked that the contest symbolized "a coming of age for Texas wines."

In 1994, Messina Hof "Angel" Late Harvest Johannisberg Riesling was the first Texas wine in ten harvests to earn a double gold medal, this time at the Tasters Guild International Wine Judging in Fort Lauderdale, Florida. At the June 1995 Los Angeles County Fair, Messina Hof won two golds: 1992 Private Reserve Cabernet Sauvignon and the 1993 Barrel Reserve Merlot.

The 1993 Slaughter-Leftwich Vineyards Sauvignon Blanc won a gold medal in the 10th Annual *Dallas Morning News* National Wine Competition, considered one of the top competitions in the country. Hill Country Cellars won a silver medal for its 1992 Merlot, and Fall Creek won a silver for its 1992 Semillon-Sauvignon Blanc. Judges tasted more than 1,400 wines from twenty-one states.

Fall Creek Vineyards' 1994 Muscat Canelli won a gold medal and Best of Show at the annual Texas Restaurant Association Texas Wine Classic.

Ste. Genevieve's Cabernet Sauvignon captured a gold medal at the 1995 San Diego National Wine Competition, and the Ste. Genevieve White Zinfandel won a gold at the 1995 New World International Wine Competition, which included over 1,800 entries worldwide.

Vineyard land in Texas is increasingly in demand. In 1995 Dale Hampton, a major California grape grower, purchased 850 acres along the San Saba River. An article in *Wine Spectator* (August 31, 1995) cited the reasons that Hampton was attracted to Texas land:

> Hampton's new vineyard cost about $1,000 per acre. At his home base near Santa Barbara, the price is at least eight times as high. A guaranteed market with Texas winery Llano Estacado makes the move even more appealing. Hampton grows fruit for such California wineries as Mondavi, Maison Deutz, Zaca Mesa, Fess Parker, and Wine World Estates.

By 1995, many Texans had developed very sophisticated palates and they expected the good wines that Texas is capable of producing. They have not been disappointed.

Fall Creek owner Ed Auler thinks the quality of Texas wines is higher than it has ever been and that it will continue to get even better. He believes the vines just need more age.

With wine, as in all refining processes, the best takes longer. And in Texas, the best just keeps on coming.

2

Modern Pioneers in the Texas Wine Industry

Bacchus opens the gates of the heart.
—Horace

The modern wine industry in Texas is indebted to many men. George Ray McEachern, extension horticulturist at Texas A&M University, is one of them. The Extension Service is the product of the Land Grant Act of 1862, a federal government decision to benefit agricultural education. The purpose was to teach agriculture, develop experimental stations for crops, and provide an extension service of technical information to the public. Texas A&M does all three, and McEachern is the grape specialist.[1] In an interview, McEachern summarized some high points of the history of Texas wines:

There were a lot of intelligent men who contributed to the Texas wine industry. T. V. Munson is legendary. His work was recognized by the U.S. Department of Agriculture and the authorities on viticulture in Montpellier, France, in the nineteenth century. He was famous for two things — the classification of the grape species, the best ever at the time, and the breeding of a very large number of new grape varieties. Several additional things were part of the Munson phenomena that have never been recorded: first, he was a promoter, and second, he was highly motivated by the economic potential of the nurs-

21

ery business. The proof of his motivation was that he always had something new to sell to the public, several new varieties each year. He was also physically strong. Munson traveled the entire Southwest on horseback and was not restricted once by illness. A&M recognized him as an outstanding viticulturist and published his paper, "Investigation and Improvement of American Grapes," even though he was not a member of the faculty. This seventy-page publication later served as the basis for his book, *Foundations of American Grape Culture.*

T. V. Munson (1843–1913) moved to Denison, Texas, in April 1876. Having completed a chemistry course in 1870 at Kentucky State Agricultural College, he visited the vineyards of his professor. They included "nearly all the then introduced varieties of American grapes." After discussing the character of the vine and fruit, he got the idea for improving grapes through cross breeding. He accepted clusters from his teacher and saved the seeds, carefully separating and labeling each one. Shortly afterwards, he moved to Nebraska, and the trial and error experiments were particularly discouraging. But eventually in Texas, as Munson said, "the flame of passion for experimentation continued to burn."

Near Denison, the limestone land was timbered with woods on the bluffs of the Red River. This higher sandy area was covered with post oak, among other trees, and the wild grapevines especially liked climbing them, hence the name Post Oak Grape. Munson recorded the presence of the Mustang Grape, Frost Grape, Bush Grape, and many others. He expressed his joy best: "I had found my grape paradise! Surely now, this is the place for experimentation with grapes."

The French honored Munson's major contribution — helping control the devastating phylloxera. He was awarded the Chevalier du Merite Agricole in the Legion of Honor and was made honorary member of the Societie des Viticulteurs de France and foreign corresponding member of the Societie National d'Agriculture de France. The phylloxera epidemic practically destroyed the world wine industry.

Munson grafted French vines onto phylloxera-resistant American rootstock and shipped these specimens to France, an act that promised a future to the demolished French wine industry. Today, Dr. Roy Renfro is director of the T. V. Munson Foundation which perpetuates the Munson varieties.

McEachern said another important name to the Texas wine industry was Ernest Mortensen.

> In the early 1930s, the Munson family turned over all of their grape variety stock to Mortensen. Mortensen grew up in an agricultural environment and was also a very smart man. After he received his master's degree from A&M, he developed the Texas A&M Winter Garden Research Center in Crystal City, Texas. His greatest motivation was to go out and find species that weren't already available in commercial horticulture. He worked with citrus and had the largest collection of date palms in the U.S.

According to McEachern, Mortensen realized that grapes would have a long vine life problem in Texas. His approach to the problem was through disease-resistant native Texas rootstocks. He selected healthy vines from the wild throughout South Texas, recognizing the importance of developing native roots. For example, when breeding or pollinating grape plants, seeds are produced and each one is unique. If there are 100 seeds planted in a row, they will produce 100 distinctly different plants. Each plant will be propagated by future cuttings off that plant — not from the seeds. Mortensen recorded his evaluations of the seedlings. The LaPryor rootstock was the product of his work.

Mortensen worked at Winter Garden from 1930 to 1952. An article in the *Texas Gardener* (November/December 1982), "The Munson Grapes; the Grapes that Lived," reported that "Mortensen was well on his way to making Texas a leader in viticulture research and grape production. But in the early 1960s [*sic*] a change in government priorities led to bulldozing the grapes, ending the program." Mortensen said it was "one of those bureaucratic things government does that is hard to understand."

McEachern has an explanation:

In the 1950s, several South Texas farmers planted Thompson seedless, a *vinifera*, for the early U.S. table grape market. They formed the Lower Rio Grande Valley Grape Growers Association, and at least five large vineyards were planted. The Peterson Brothers at Rio Grande City, the Trautmann Brothers at Laredo, and O. P. Leonard at Crystal City were earlier planters. Unfortunately, the South Texas vineyards died from three things: freeze, cotton root rot, and Pierce's disease. This eliminated the table grape industry in the Lower Rio Grande in the late 1950s. Also, all the major horticulturists in the state were aware of this, and it had a great deal to do with the philosophy toward grape growing in Texas. Extension service horticulturist Bluefford Hancock and Professor Fred R. Brison did not want to lead people in the wrong direction agriculturally. Based on the failed vineyards, they couldn't recommend commercial grapes to farmers.

In 1937, A&M established a Fruit Investigation Laboratory at Montague, Texas, with grape research as the primary goal. McEachern elaborated:

It had premium soil, and Uiel Randolph was hired to run it. He grew grapes with ease at Montague in the early 1940s and throughout the 1950s. This was simultaneous to the South Texas project. Looking back, it is difficult to know how many grape varieties were grown at Montague, but it was essentially all the American hybrids and over 100 French/American hybrids. Randolph did an outstanding job between 1942 and 1962 and had an outstanding grape research program. In 1962, A&M decided to discontinue its research on grapes because in the later years there were very few requests for grape information. This was also following the South Texas table grape failure. Randolph published his findings, however, in Experiment Station reports — mostly on American hybrids — so the records are good.[2]

During the same period that the South Texas and Montague experiments were being conducted, a horticulturist named Bill Cook was working for the Missouri-Pacific Railroad. At that time railroads often had staff members who advised farmers on the feasibility of products that offered potential shipment business for the line. According to McEachern,

> Cook became excited about grapes, and he more than anyone else in Texas became interested in rootstocks. He was heavily involved in the Lower Rio Grande grape project, recognizing the economic potential for South Texas's table grape production. But he also recognized the importance of rootstock in the control of disease. His major effort was to find a root system resistant to cotton root rot and nematodes that was compatible with *vinifera* varieties. Cook went into South Texas fields that were heavily infested with cotton root rot and planted thousands of grape seeds in the hope of finding a rootstock seedling that would work for both diseases. He field tested them for cotton root rot, and Dr. Walter Thanes of A&M evaluated them for nematodes — a microscopic worm that bores into the root and obstructs nutrition and water flow to the plant. Cook recognized several profound things, one of which was "practically all the wild grape seedlings, particularly the Mustang, show a high degree of resistance, if not immunity, to both cotton root rot and nematodes." Then the industry died in the 1950s. But three men — Cook, Randolph, and Mortensen — were ahead of their time.[3]

There was a vineyard revolution in Texas during the 1970s. Actually, it was going on all over the United States. Texans were slower to develop because they were determined to be thorough researchers. As a result, McEachern thinks they did a better job.

> It turns out that California discovered wine in the 1960s and America discovered wine in the 1970s. If you had not been part of the early phenomena, it's hard to imagine what happened. Every state in the United States experienced some sort of vineyard expansion. It was less significant in Texas in the early days than other states; Washington, Oregon, Idaho, and Michigan just to mention a few. For some reason, Arizona, New Mexico, and Texas did not proliferate as fast, but I never apologize about the slow progress of Texas. I think being deliberate is a big part of why we have succeeded.

In viticulture you have a very high probability of failure. It's a very complex high-tech form of agriculture. The opportunities for failure are greater than for any other crop. Fortunately, we had a few Texas families that went about it slowly, deliberately, methodically, and in an exacting way—in small units. For example, Ed Auler put in 120 vines to experiment with, and Bobby Cox did his homework at the A&M Experimental Station in Lubbock before he ever planted a grape. Bob Oberhelman researched grapes for six years before he planted.

If I had to pick those who first recognized the potential for commercial wine grapes in Texas, it would be Clint McPherson and Robert Reed, both professors at Texas Tech. They collaborated on putting in a small vineyard and called it "Sagmore" because their wires sagged more than anyone else's, but the vines and their wines were good.

McEachern explained that Texans realized early on that they could grow American grapes, such as the Munson varieties. However, they also realized that a wine industry could not be built from those grapes. In the early years, the saving grace was going to be the French/American hybrids. The *vinifera* wine grape had not arrived.

In 1973, McEachern received a grant for a trial demonstration across the state involving twelve grape varieties. Thirty test plots were planted. Each site received three Americans, three hybrids, three *viniferas*, and three varieties of the grower's choice. He described the progress of the project:

These demonstrations were established from Fort Stockton to Texarkana and from Abilene to San Antonio. For the most part, about half of the vineyards died in only two years. But Auler's vineyard was something else. The Aurelia, a hybrid, produced seventeen tons per acre the fourth year. We still did not know which way we wanted to go—American, *vinifera*, or hybrid—because we were still influenced by our cloud of failure from cotton root rot, Pierce's disease, and freeze. As I said, at that time everyone had planted hybrids, but they knew what *viniferas* could do and most growers planted a few just to watch them. One grower in Lubbock, Darrell Boepple, wanted to plant the grapes that would bring the highest price, so he planted six acres of Cabernet Sauvignon. Bobby Cox made wine from it in 1979, and Leon Adams [author and authority on American wines] tasted it and said "You Texans just may have a chance." At that time there was pressure from a few who insisted we ought to be planting *vinifera* — Kim McPherson, who had gone to work for his dad at Llano Estacado, said we should get rid of everything except *vinifera*. Gretchen Glasscock was willing to spend whatever it took to grow Sauvignon Blanc. She loved *vinifera* and she wanted *vinifera*. By 1980, growers all over West Texas were watching their own experimental plots of *vinifera*. At Texas A&M we had to learn with the industry. There were many successful vineyards across the state: Bobby Smith, Clint McPherson, Ed Auler, the A&M Cooperatives, University of Texas, the Experiment Stations; all the early boys did the same thing, learned with the industry, and grew one step at a time.

Simultaneous to these plantings and the development, another important thing happened. A young man named Ron Perry wrote a feasibility study at the Texas Agricultural Experiment Station at College Station. It was good, according to McEachern, and positive.

Ron Perry analyzed the soils, climate, water, and diseases for Texas. Later, he and Dr. William Lipe established outstanding research vineyards of excellent experimental design including three rootstocks and sixty varieties at El Paso, Lubbock, Uvalde, and Junction. These research vineyards also encouraged people, and it fanned the fire of the Texas wine dream. Dr. Lipe is a full-time grape researcher at Lubbock and has expanded the grape research to include freeze tolerance, growth regulations, rootstocks, and pest management.

Another positive factor in the 1970s was Val Verde Winery. Tommy Qualia enlisted the aid of wine consultant Enrique Ferro, and they revamped the winery. Qualia put in new stainless steel tanks, refrigeration units, and a new press. The result was an excellent port. In the early part of the same decade, Dr. Roy Mitchell of the Chemistry Department at Texas Tech conducted a research program on winemaking from the first commercial vineyards in the Lubbock area. He also provided assistance to the early winemakers in Texas. McEachern said:

> The single greatest vineyard project in Texas was the University of Texas Lands Department of Surface Interest Project in far West Texas. I can remember the first time I met Billy Carr, manager of the Surface Interests of the UT System in West Texas. I've never met a man more excited about anything! He wanted to talk to me about grapes. And talk we did. I guess the rest is history. But it's important to realize that a lot of decisions were made by Billy Carr — not all at once — but over a six-year period. Fortunately, each step was positive up to and including the decision to plant a thousand-acre commercial vineyard. Carr built an excellent staff of Dr. Charles McKinney, Gene Drennan, and Roy Mitchell. They planted three experimental vineyards on university land and together made very good *vinifera* wine. Then the contract was made with Richardson Gill to form Ste. Genevieve with partners Richter, Cordier, and Anthony Sanchez. I believe Ste. Genevieve is good for Texas. With the volume of wine produced and the good vintages, Ste. Genevieve will establish the name of the Texas wine industry around the world.

The Texas Grape Growers Association is dear to the heart of McEachern. He said it was by no means an insignificant part of the industry; in fact, he called it the unifying mechanism that pulled everybody together during the formative years.

> I gave a speech at the October 1973 meeting of the Texas Fruit Growers Conference titled "The Potential for Wine Production in Texas in 1973." There was a reporter there whom I never met, but he sent out an AP story on my speech. Following that story I began receiving fifty letters a month on how to grow grapes in Texas. A special half-day session on grapes was held at the 1974 Texas Fruit Conference. About thirty grape growers attended. Afterwards, we held a planning meeting in room 110 of the

Plant Science Building. The people in that room later proved to be the leaders of the new Texas grape industry. We talked about grapes for more than six hours. At the close of that meeting, Clint McPherson asked me to form an association for the Texas Grape Growers. So I did.[4]

Looking back, McEachern credits the good wine that had been made as the main motivation.

When we learned that we didn't have to grow only hybrids of American grapes, it was a good surprise. But when people from outside tasted the early Texas *vinifera* and said, "Hey, this is good, I'm surprised!" it was wonderful. All of us involved in the Texas industry also realized over a period of years that our wines were getting better. Today we realize, along with wine authorities in Europe and California, that the potential for Texas wine is great.

Today, the wine and food industries are growing together through their mutual support and dependence. In 1985, Susan Auler, co-owner of Fall Creek Vineyards, brought together a group of interested persons to create the Texas Hill Country Wine and Food Festival. The author (Sarah Jane English) was a charter council and board member and one of a small core group — Susan Auler, Cindy Stone, Tricia Zeigler, Jeannine Stroth — who expended tremendous energy and effort to launch the event in 1986. That year 20,000 personalized invitations were sent.

"Texas experienced a proliferation of new restaurants in the 1970s," Susan explained, "and simultaneously a Texas wine industry was emerging. I felt the time was right to focus on the exciting new developments in wine and food in Texas. Basically, we wanted to focus on the Hill Country as a viticultural region and additionally on Texas food products, Texas cooking and Texas chefs, hence the first Texas Hill Country Wine and Food Festival was inaugurated in 1986." (The festival benefits KMFA, a nonprofit, listener-supported, classical music radio station, and KLRU-TV, a public television station, both in Austin.)

Involving the Texas Beef Industry Council in the Hill

Country Festival was a natural, and in 1987 it joined the project to add tremendously to the volunteer effort. Anne Anderson, executive director of the Council, summarized its involvement: "In many ways the festival and the beef industry are good companions. Beef is a trendy food again. It's bred to be leaner and even more healthful. When we promote beef at the festival, the chefs involved come up with new and exciting recipes. Participants come to learn about food and wine, and it's an ideal medium for the modern beef industry."

The year 1988 marked the inauguration of "Who's Who in Food and Wine in Texas." It honored the arrival of Texas personalities who were making noteworthy contributions to the food and wine industries.

Trends continue to shape and change lifestyles and food styles, but fine food and wine doubtlessly will be a constant in the lives of discriminating Texans.

NOTES

1. "In 1883, Frank Qualia planted a vineyard at Del Rio," McEachern said. "His son, Louis Qualia, took over in 1935 and managed the vineyard until 1975. He told me that they attempted to grow over 100 varieties of grapes and only those resistant to Pierce's disease survived. So after ninety years, the varieties for Val Verde Winery were limited to Lenoir, Herbemont, Ellen Scott, and Champanel."

According to McEachern, Texas A&M has been invaluable to Texas grape production from the state's earliest days. In 1888, T. L. Brunk planted ninety-six varieties at College Station. In 1898, the research vineyard was expanded by R. H. Price and H. Ness to 170 varieties, including all commercial species. All *Vitis lubrusca* varieties had difficulty and all *Vitis vinifera* varieties or their hybrids were short-lived. Today it is realized that the problems could have been Pierce's disease, cotton root rot, iron chlorosis, freeze, black rot, nematodes, and/or poor soil.

2. Mortensen and Randolph were recognized many years later for their outstanding contributions to the Texas grape industry by the Texas Grape Growers Association at the second annual meeting in San Antonio, 1978. Together they published over thirty research reports on Texas grapes, their finest being the

Texas Agricultural Experiment Station Circular No. 89 — "Grape Production in Texas, June 1940."

3. The rootstock research of the early station is of great value today, according to McEachern. New plant propagation techniques of the 1980s will allow the Texas industry to utilize the work of the early researchers. A good rootstock will need to be resistant to cotton root rot, phylloxera, nematodes, iron chlorosis, and cold injury, as well as produce quality fruit in an economic volume.

4. Over the next thirty-two months, three organizational meetings were held, according to McEachern: two at San Angelo and one at Junction, and the early commercial grape growers of Texas organized what is now the Texas Grape Growers Association. The first annual meeting was held March 1, 1977, in Austin, Texas.

"The Texas Grape Growers Association provided a method of communication on viticulture and oenology between growers and professionals," McEachern said. "The TGGA as a group could bring people into Texas who were experienced in viticulture and oenology. We couldn't have done that on an individual basis."

3

Texas Hill Country Wines

For in the hand of the Lord there is a cup,
and the wine is red.

— Psalms 75:8

There's an undefinable magic about the Texas Hill Country. It's like opening an old family trunk full of unexpected treasures. Texans are imbued with the magic. Listening to one talk about his land is similar to discovering a new literary genre, something midway between poetic and romantic. The character of the land is personified in one breath, and the unpredictable horror of nature's surprises is cursed in the next. Nonetheless, the captivating Hill Country inspires.

There's color in the hills. Slices of salmon soil lay next to vanilla-colored land, dividing it immediately, and consequently, dramatically. One color comes from granite and the other from limestone. In the spring the hues multiply. Fields of wildflowers paint the country in an undulating and continuous rainbow of purple mountain laurel, bluebonnets, red Indian paintbrush, and the golden groundsel.

Stones color the Hill Country, too. Like a reverse human aging effect, huge, monumental stones have been smoothed over the years by the elements. They appear to have had earth packed around them protectively, commanding a guarded respect that the permanence of nature deserves, yet touting their longevity over more fragile things.

The land has a fickle personality, often rough, coarse, dry, and impenetrable, but at the next turn are rolling green hills where underground springs give way to visible water- ways of coolness. Perhaps the most incredible feature is the Llano Uplift. The name refers to a geological formation, but in layman's terms it is a big rock, a huge piece of granite seventy miles across and 1,000 feet deep. Through the years rains have washed in rivers and helped to create the valleys and rich soils — among the oldest and most varied in Texas. Mineral deposits are a normal composition of this structure and have led many to search for the hidden gold and silver mines purported to exist here. But the Hill Country is endowed with an equally rich treasure of nature in its grapes. There are several wineries in the region, and many of them are located among their own vineyards.

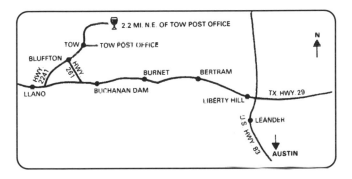

Fall Creek Vineyards

Fall Creek is one of the estate vineyards that is part of the Texas Hill Country. The ranch of which it is a part has its own legends and mysteries, and owners Ed and Susan Auler enjoy sharing its history. The idea for the vineyards and win- ery began in 1973 when the Aulers were traveling through France. Ed noticed a similarity between parts of the French wine country and the Texas Hill Country where the ranch is located. Auler said:

> In a real sense, I suppose Fall Creek started long before
> that trip. We had a desire to do something with the land

because Texas is a very special place to us, the Hill Country is a very special part of Texas, and Fall Creek is a very special part of the Hill Country. It has been in our family for four generations, but beyond that it has been occupied by civilization for about 10,000 years. Fall Creek has some of the most fantastic history. Much of it is documented, some is fragmented, and a lot is merely speculation, but it's all fascinating.

There's a legend of buried treasure on the ranch which derives from traces of silver and gold deposits long known to old-timers. There never has been enough of the minerals to merit mining, but it's part of the land's romantic heritage. Other stories concern Indians. The Tonkawa lived on the ranch for several thousand years, and it was a perennial site for the Comanches. Also, branches of the old cattle trails went through Fall Creek, and in the middle of the nineteenth century, a place on the ranch was the first county seat for Llano County after it was carved from Bexar District, Gillespie County, in 1856.

Background on the land and its ultimate use for grape growing is offered by Auler:

As far as learning to love the land, I grew up with it. It's sort of in the blood. Just as a lot of children, I hunted different rocks, searched for arrowheads, looked for game, and later on I worked a little on the ranch and then I worked more, and then the ranch got to be more work.

We raised livestock. Unfortunately, it's more a way of life than it is a means of income, although some years are good enough to give you the incentive, if not the means, to make it through the bad years. In my family, each generation always acquired more land and did something different with it. My father believed that you either ought to do something better than everybody else or do something different. He was the first person to introduce Angus cattle into the Hill Country. I can remember the day he took those black cows up there. People were standing along the roadside shaking their heads. They told him: "You just don't raise anything but white-faced Herefords in the Texas Hill Country." But being a physician, with a strong interest in genetics, he not only brought good

black cattle, but conducted a breeding program of the
type that gave us about as good a herd of black cattle as
any in the state. . . .

I wanted to keep the cattle ranch going, and I've always considered ways to improve it. We thought about
raising peaches, apples — something in addition to cattle.
Then the idea for grapes hit me. I think I was standing in
the curve of the road at Clos de Vougeot. I looked up at
the escarpment above and then down at the soil and then
across the valley. There was granite on one side and limestone on the other, and I thought it looked like the Texas
Hill Country. In 1974, the bottom dropped out of the
cattle market and I decided to plant vines.

Auler visited with the Llano County agent, John
Kuykendall, and inquired about other projects just beginning in the state. Then he contacted George Ray McEachern
at Texas A&M and began to gather literature on the subjects
of drainage, likely vineyard locations, possible problems,
and so forth. McEachern recommended several varieties of
grapevines, and the test plot was established in 1975 with
nine French/American hybrids and two *vinifera*. Auler expounded:

By the end of the first year, we had growth runners fifty-
one feet long. The difference between the two longest
runners on one vine was ninety-seven feet. George Ray
did some research, and to the best of his findings it was
the most incredible vigor that had ever been seen or
heard of, in any country including Algeria, and they were
all on their own rootstocks. We had to wait until 1978,
however, to find out if the fruit would make good wine,
because big, pretty vines don't insure success. In fact,
some of the best wines are made from stressed, less
vigorous vines.

Many of the people Auler visited with were not very
optimistic. They told him *vinifera* wouldn't grow in Texas,
and hybrids probably wouldn't grow either. He also heard
that his vines wouldn't produce enough sugar in Texas, but
if he did get enough sugar, the acid would be too low and
the pH too high.

"It turned out that in most all the varieties we harvested in 1977, the sugar/acid/pH balance was either very good or acid high — which is a good problem if you're going to have a problem. At that point we felt that good wines could be made," he said.

Vines usually seek nutrients deep in the soil. It may take years for roots to reach a level that ultimately offers the flavors considered desirable for wine. Auler read and studied and received knowledgeable help from The University of Texas, Texas A&M, and Texas Tech. As the test plot was watched, Auler and the consultants shared notes and compared what was happening.

> We told each other what we knew, and in almost every instance one of us would know something that the others didn't. We consulted Dr. Petrucci of Fresno who was one of the earliest believers in Texas wine grapes. He came down here to tell us what we were doing wrong or right, but usually was more complimentary than critical. Once we saw we had the fruit, our goal was to build a winery, not just grow grapes, and our commitment was to extract the absolute best quality we could.

At that time, Texas didn't have a designated wine region. For example, temperatures for vineyards are based on daily readings of fifty degrees Fahrenheit and classified accordingly. The tables are called the "heat summation." It is a complicated process, but it measures the number of days that a region provides the necessary warmth for vines to grow during the four-month season. A daily mean temperature for a thirty-day month might be seventy degrees, or twenty degrees above the minimum fifty degrees required. The degrees above the required fifty are multiplied by the number of days in the month. The resulting figure gives the region a heat summation of 600 "degree days," which places it between Region III and Region IV.

Region I	62–65 daily average
Region II	65–68 daily average
Region III	68–70 daily average
Region IV	70–74 daily average
Region V	74–80 daily average

Auler described the precarious beginnings of the Texas wine industry:

> We didn't know if we'd be a five or a three, like the south of France or like northern Italy. No one knew. The only history we had of viticulture in Texas was one of early failure by settlers who planted the wrong vines in the wrong areas. Many who landed at Galveston brought *vinifera* with them. They planted them in southeast Texas and they almost immediately died. As they moved west they were either too busy fighting to survive on the frontier or the memory of failure was too fresh. Of some twenty or so wineries that existed before Prohibition, the best evidence we have shows that they were making native American wine, which by today's standards would be quite inferior. At that time, those people were probably satisfied with them. *Viniferas* weren't tried in other areas, and of course they didn't have the hybrids. But if those people had tried these types of grapes in the Texas Hill Country, the High Plains, and the Trans-Pecos, Texas might have been the leading wine-producing state long before California. History didn't roll that way. I think that's what the Texas wine industry is really all about now. It's sort of the rebirth of an industry that was never quite born back in the 1800s.

The Aulers have dedicated almost as much time to building Texas' wine industry as they have to Fall Creek. Ed served the first two years as president of the Texas Grape Growers Association, a position he was elected to once again in 1986. He has lobbied for legislation beneficial to the industry, and he serves as chairman of the Winery Council, which he organized in 1985. His expertise as a Texas winemaker, along with his legal background, has made Auler the chief spokesman for the Texas wine industry since the mid-1970s. His dedication and efforts have spurred the projection that Texas will be the number-two wine-producing state in the United States by the end of the 1990s.

Truly, viticulture is one of the bright spots on the economic horizon in Texas. So is Susan Auler. In 1985, Susan took on the tremendous project of organizing and working with a committee to produce the Texas Hill Country Wine

and Food Festival, a spring event that celebrates the beauty
and bounty of the Hill Country. The three-day, annual affair,
which includes seminars, wine tastings, food booths, fes-
tivities, and international participants, is open to the public.

The Aulers have contributed immeasurably to the renaissance of the Texas wine industry. Invitations to showcase their Fall Creek wines at winemaker dinners, wine and
food symposiums, and at benefit dinners around the United
States are constant. The Aulers participated in the "James
Beard Meals on Wheels" benefit in New York with top
American chefs and winemakers in April 1988. Then Susan
served as a panelist for a Chardonnay tasting at the Aspen/
Snowmass Wine and Food Classic, June 1988. The Ameri-
can Institute of Wine and Food once again invited the
Aulers to showcase Fall Creek wines at the Third Annual
Wines of USA at the Windows on the World, New York.

By the late 1970s, Auler's test plot of vines was among
the first of the reviving industry, and his work was significant to many.

> We made some experimental wine off the first harvest
> that we thought was fairly good at the time. I'd hate to
> taste some of it now, but others commented favorably
> and it influenced us to work to open a small winery in
> 1978. Then we were totally hailed out that year, and I feel
> it was probably a blessing in disguise.

The damage by the hailstorm gave Auler time to
reevaluate his vineyards as well as operating procedures. He
opened a small winery in 1979, one with a 3,000-gallon capacity in a 1,000-square-foot building. The intention was to
make the best quality wine from the Fall Creek Vineyard
grapes.

> The hybrids and the three *viniferas* were doing well. But
> the skeptics had told us for so long that we couldn't grow
> *viniferas* in Texas that we believed them. So we concen-
> trated on the French/American hybrids. I have nothing
> per se against them. They're just not *vinifera*. But the best
> hybrids are never going to be as good as the best *vinifera*
> varieties. Anyway, we thought this was the best we could

do, so we concentrated primarily on Villard Blanc and Aurora.

Something else happened in 1980 that Auler also considers a blessing in disguise. The incident had to do with disease. The chief disease problems for grapes are nematodes, cotton root rot, Pierce's disease, and phylloxera. One day he walked into the Emerald Riesling vineyard and everything was fine. Three days later, fifteen vines were dead. A root analysis showed that there was a massive infiltration of cotton root rot.

> It turned out that we had a row of four-year-old Champanels growing right straight through the middle of the dying Emerald Riesling. After talking to Ernest Mortensen and Tommy Qualia, I learned Champanel had indeed shown immunity to cotton root rot and probably phylloxera and nematodes as well. I decided to graft everything onto Champanel, and since the few *viniferas* we had were performing as well or better than our hybrids, I felt there was no need to be growing hybrids if I was going to graft our vines onto the Champanel rootstock. So I planted Chenin Blanc, Zinfandel, more Carnelian and Ruby Cabernet that next year — all on Champanel.

Two years later the early fruits of that endeavor were rewarding. The varietal character of the *vinifera* was showing on the grafted plants, and the growth characteristics of the *vinifera* grafted onto Champanel in terms of bud-break and dormancy were initially identical with the *vinifera* themselves. It was so successful that all of Fall Creek's sixty-five acres are now planted with *vinifera* grafted onto Champanel. Under the supervision of Tom Barkley, master-degree horticulturist and vineyard manager, Fall Creek is extensively propagating the rootstock and custom-grafting vines for other growers with similar rootstock needs all across the Southwest. When Auler initially shifted the whole emphasis to *viniferas*, he planted the best-known varieties — Chardonnay and Cabernet Sauvignon, varieties previously thought impossible to grow in the Hill Country. At that time the decision was made to build a major winery. Auler explained:

> We didn't want a feasibility study. We wanted something
> that would last for generations, something we could add
> onto. When we built the structure we tried to accom-
> modate the best Old World winemaking techniques with
> the best California innovative technology and our Texas
> fruit. That's not to say we tried to mold Texas wines. We
> wanted to perfect whatever character the grapes imparted
> to our wines. So we built a structure that would accommo-
> date this philosophy, be compatible with our environ-
> ment, and also reflect the existing wine world — something
> that would hopefully give wine its place in Texas.

Susan Auler did the same thing in helping to design and decorate the winery. Her selections include rare French antiques that once belonged to Louis Pasteur as well as Texas objets d'art found on the ranch. Ed said she did a grand job and attributes much of the success at Fall Creek to her tireless efforts in numerous projects. The place reflects the best from three regions — French antiquities, Texas artifacts, and California-style contemporary touches.

The winery was constructed in 1982. Additions were made in 1986, 1987, and 1988, and vineyards have steadily increased. But besides the building and the test plots, Auler has been a pioneer in the revitalization of the Texas wine industry in other respects.

> We've had a lot of problems along the way. For one, the
> vineyards were located in a dry area, and it was against
> the law to make wine there. Dr. Bobby Smith of La Buena
> Vida was as concerned as I was because he had planted
> vineyards in a dry area, too. So Bobby and I drafted a bill
> and did the work on it. The bill passed the Senate without
> a dissenting vote, and only about two people abstained in
> the House. The governor signed it, and it was legal for us
> to make wine in a dry area. We certainly didn't solve all
> the legal intricacies that plague our wine industry, but at
> least that was a first step.
>
> In that respect we were pacesetters, and all the
> people who said we'd never get any positive action from

the legislature — those who said it couldn't be done — are the very ones asking us now how to do it. First Black Angus; now wine grapes.

Fall Creek has had a plan for growth. In 1985, there were forty-five acres under vines with sixty-five in 1989 and seventy-five acres in 1990. The winery has a 60,000-gallon capacity. Auler said they don't have specific growth numbers in mind except two. He wants to grow as big as possible as long as quality is not compromised, and he never wants supply to exceed demand.

We're fortunate in that we run out of wine very quickly. We hope we have that kind of problem for a long, long time. We haven't begun to tap the Texas market, and now other states — New York, California, Washington, D.C. — are asking for our wine. The British are importing it. From a marketing standpoint, we seem to have a guardian angel. Our wine goes in one door and out the other. We can't do anything but count our blessings.

We improve our quality each year. Annually in January I look at our previous year's wine and realize how much I like it, but I realize the newer vintage is so much better. We've done that each year, and we know that one year that won't happen. But our vines are getting older, our technology is improving, and we're solving some of the infinite parameters that are involved with wine — so we feel the best is yet to come. The problem is that there's such lag time between changing just one factor and the time you get to evaluate it.

Research has shown that the problems of individual factors are compounded by the interrelationships among factors. Texas is fortunate to have the history of other wine industries as a resource. Auler believes Texas is where California was twenty years ago.

No one took California seriously twenty years ago. Everyone takes them seriously today. If my assumption is correct, in the not distant future we should be in pretty much of an equilibrium with what they can do on most varieties. And I think that's exciting — not just for winemakers like me who have pioneered for others, but for the state because it needs a new economy. We need something else to do in the rural areas.

This is an extremely labor-intensive industry that can provide employment. There's an incredible enthusiasm that goes along with this industry, whether people are picking grapes, working in the laboratories, or marketing the wine. It seems to be contagious and pervasive, and it's very enjoyable to see people be so enthusiastic about what they're doing. I think the industry will help the state from a tourism standpoint, from a revenue standpoint, and also be a new base for taxation. It's a clean industry and a healthy beverage used properly. As Louis Pasteur said, "It's the most healthful and hygienic of all beverages."

The joy shows in the wine. Fall Creek wines have won many awards over the years. The 1983 Sauvignon Blanc and Chenin Blanc were chosen as wines from thirty selected American wineries to be served at "Taste of America," an event held in conjunction with the 1985 presidential inauguration. The Sauvignon Blanc, Emerald Riesling, Chenin Blanc, and Carnelian have won medals at various competitions since 1983, including a bronze medal for the 1984 Emerald Riesling at the 1985 San Francisco Fair National Wine Competition. It won a gold medal at the Best of Texas Competition in 1985.

In recent times there has been an oversupply of wine. Benevolent weather has made crops plentiful. Technology has advanced disease control. In addition, Auler sees a trend toward greater numbers of quality producers because quality will be essential for survival in the wine business.

At Fall Creek we not only want to be a survivor, we want to be an aggressive player. If people like Leon Adams, Petrucci, and Balzer tell us we have the ability to make world-class wines, then what we want to make is world-class wines. We have no desire to play in the jug market. If you don't set your sights on the best markets, you're never going to make it. Others say we're on the right track. We may not be at the top of the ladder yet, but we're a long way from the bottom, and we're not going to take a breath until Fall Creek is among the very best wine available on the market.

While beginning wine drinkers usually start with a light, slightly sweet, white wine and progress to drier whites and then red wines, many people first tasted Texas wines because they were a novelty. It has been explained that Americans grow up with sweetened iced tea and cold drinks and have a natural inclination toward sweet beverages. Some Texas wines have been made to satisfy that taste, but Auler explains that Fall Creek wines represented other considerations.

> I think we make wines that appeal to a fairly large number of tastes. I don't like the term sweet for our wines, and I don't really think any of them is considered sweet. Yet, our Chenin Blanc, which has 1.8 residual sugar, has a tremendously broad appeal, much more than I would ever have imagined. While our primary thrust is to be competitive with the best and most competitive wines, we're going to make wines that have a wide appeal too, but we have no intention of ever catering to the mass market. We're going to make the best wines we can. I use the plural pronoun because Susan is my indispensable partner in all aspects of the business.
>
> We have consistently produced award-winning wines. Fall Creek had more gold medal-winning wines than any other Texas winery in 1987 Texas wine competitions. This fact and the successes of the other Hill Country vineyards puts the Hill Country at the top of the list of premium wine-growing regions in Texas. Research is being conducted to register these exceptional microclimates as Texas appellations.

Challenges stimulate Auler, and a combination that is particularly gratifying is one that requires working with both his mind and his hands. Flying airplanes and making wine are two such endeavors — and the reasons why he practices less law and channels more of his time and effort into making wine.

> It's rewarding in that respect, but the extra added rewards have been greater.
> I love the outdoors and the country. I could almost hibernate at times. But I'm a people person too, usually more so individually than collectively. But it's incredible

the number of different things that are involved in a winery operation. Not only do you have to be a chemist, a
plumber, a horticulturist, an electrician, a physicist, sales-
man, accountant, and lawyer, but also promotionally
minded, and on and on. The wine industry has so many
tangential things of a public relations nature that most
people don't begin to comprehend, and most of them are
truly fun. They take you to a wide diversity of places for a
number of reasons, and that in itself has a very broaden-
ing aspect. But the people you meet, the consumers, are
some of the finest in the world. They're people who have
virtually nothing else in common but an interest in wine.

The history and geography of the ranch and Fall Creek
Vineyards fascinate Texana buffs and oenologists equally.
Located in Llano County on the northwest shores of Lake
Buchanan, the land has several hundred springs that feed
Fall Creek, a stream that rambles for thirteen miles through
the Auler property. Originally, the water fell over a 150-foot
bluff into a pool beside the Colorado River, hence the
name; however, when Lake Buchanan was created the water
level rose, and the waterfall is now about 100 feet tall.

The vineyard's beauty and abundance of history are
cited by Auler:

> Fall Creek is probably about the prettiest stream in Texas.
> Many of the springs not only never go dry, but they never
> change their flow — no matter what. The main spring
> comes out of the Ellenburger limestone formation, which
> is the same formation that at 16,000 feet out in West
> Texas produces oil and gas. But on the upslope it's
> producing the purest of water. The waterfall was one of
> the major archaeological sites of The University of Texas
> in the 1930s. At one time a good portion of the Texas
> Memorial Museum artifacts came out of Fall Creek sites.
> The numerous caves are of interest, too — pictographs
> and burials and the evidence of an interchange of cul-
> tures.

Many of the old cattle trails wandered through Fall
Creek. The Chisholm Trail actually had several branches:
eastern, central, and western. The western portion traveled

up the river bed and another branch connected with the Goodnight-Loving Trail. These crossed on Fall Creek. Many of the old signs painted on the bluffs to give distances are still visible, as are the ruts cut into the rocks by heavily laden wagons. Though the terrain was not well suited for wagon travel, it proved to be prime land for grape vineyards. Auler explained:

> There are at least three major geological regions and maybe seven or eight subregions that converge at Fall Creek: the Llano Uplift, the Edwards Plateau, and the Cross Timbers. From a grape standpoint, it's very influential—in terms of the type of soil. The Llano Uplift, which is about the oldest rock on earth, goes under the ground about where the Edwards Plateau comes out—right on the edge of our vineyards. The soil is made for growing grapes.
>
> Another factor is the prevailing southerly winds which blow across Buchanan and give us rapid nighttime cooling effect. In other words, we have a very definitive microclimate. We're hot in the day but cool at night—like the High Plains and Trans-Pecos. Once you get west of the Balcones Fault, the relative humidity drops off rapidly. The difference between the climate in Austin and at Fall Creek is remarkable, and it's only sixty-five air miles. A typical Austin day is ninety-five degrees high and seventy-five degrees low and fifty percent humidity. That would be a 100-degree day at Fall Creek, but the low that evening would be sixty-eight degrees with a relative humidity twenty to twenty-five percent. When you combine that with the rapid nighttime cooling effect off Buchanan, the grapes can retain the acid and build up their sugars a bit slower than they otherwise might. As a result, we began pulling up our hybrids and planting primarily Chardonnay, and that's basically a Region I or II grape. In fact, we now have an experimental plot of ten different clones of Chardonnay, all grafted onto Champanel. This experimental plot, which is being carefully conducted and monitored by Tom Barkley, should reveal not only which clones are best adapted to Fall Creek Vineyards but also should provide significant data for other viticulturists in similar grape-growing regions.

Good soil and a healthy climate don't insure a good vintage. Perfect ones are infrequent. In those fortunate years, even an amateur winemaker could probably make an impressive wine. Most years are not like that, however, and the winemaker has to deal with an incredible number of unknown factors. It's so complicated that no one ever understands it all, but Auler says part of the job is to "capture the clues."

Fall Creek is still revealing clues about its land and history. The vineyards are basically sandy loam on the edge of granite with red and yellow clay undulating from three to six feet deep. The Texas Hill Country, however, abounds in types of soils. Between Llano and Junction, a distance of about seventy-five air miles, there are approximately seventy-five soils: shale, chalk, lime, black, sandy loam, and granite to name a few. Dramatic changes in elevation, presence of water, and wind direction and location give the region multiple microclimates.

The climate isn't the only dramatic feature of Fall Creek; its history is just as interesting. For example, one of the largest live oak trees in the United States is growing on Fall Creek property. Auler said the old tree was the first site for holding court in Llano County.

> The reason the spot was picked was because it was near the cattle trails, made by people who had fought their way through the hostile Indians and primitive, rough country. They could just move slightly off the trail to be under that tree and hold court. It was named the Procter tree because a man named Procter was hung from it. After that, there were two treaties signed with the Indians under it. We can tell it's probably over 1,000 years old by comparing it to a similar tree near Leakey on the Sabinal River which is reputed to be the second largest live oak in Texas. The Fall Creek tree properly measured four feet above ground level has a circumference of thirty-four feet. That puts it in close competition for the largest live oak tree in existence. We're planning to put picnic tables underneath it so visitors to Fall Creek can have lunch beneath it.

There are other treasures at Fall Creek. While the Indian burial mounds are left undisturbed, artifacts have been collected from the vineyards. According to Auler, some of the best points and knives in his collection have been found among the vines of Chenin Blanc and Emerald Riesling right in front of the winery. The land does not give them up readily. Only after plowing and a good rain do the pieces become visible. Actually, the retrieval of anything from Texas land is in keeping with demands. Texas earth seems to have a tough philosophy that makes struggle important. Auler sums it up well:

> People were willing to fight to settle here, and I think partly because of the beauty. The land asks so much of you in order to yield up its treasures. I get the impression that other agricultural and mining areas have something there for the taking. But there's very little you can do in Texas that doesn't put up a fight. It's harder to do anything here than most any place else, and yet the rewards have proven to be greater for those willing to put up with the inconveniences. Not many years ago, no one would have tried to farm on the High Plains or have taken an oil rig west of the Pecos River. The land gives an extra dimension to the challenge, and the Texans who did were special people. I think we're doing that with grapes.

The loving pride Texans feel for their land and history is no secret. Their outspoken testimony about the wonder of things Texan has established a worldwide reputation for them. Certainly, part of that devotion derives from a personal toil to create something, and the more difficult it is, the greater the pride in achievement. Part of man's nature seems to be the pride of a successful struggle. The greater the struggle, the more rewarding the conquest and the dearer the prize. Texans have always believed the Lone Star state had a unique endowment, and sharing the land gives Texans a touch of that uniqueness. Ed Auler is adding a successful chapter to Texas history and continuing the proud tradition that perhaps only Texans can truly understand.

Disaster struck Fall Creek Vineyards on December 23, 1991. On that date the temperature fell to -12°F. Lake

Buchanan and Fall Creek were frozen solid, and so were many grapevines. Initially about 20% of the vines were killed outright. The other 80% were alive and were thought to have survived. Time would show, however, that most of the surviving vines were severely damaged, with retarded growth, and greatly reduced crop yield. Many of those "surviving" vines died the next year or two.

"To go forward we had to make some fundamental decisions," said Ed Auler. "First, we decided to replant our vineyards in stages. In so doing we adopted a new trellis system called the lyre system."

That system has proven itself an excellent one for vigorous vines so that leaf-grape ratio can be maximized, crop yield can be bigger, harvesting made easier, and vineyard maintenance less costly. Replanting began in 1993, to continue through 1996.

During the replanting, Fall Creek Vineyards has gone from a situation of "growing 80% and buying 20% to a situation of growing 20% and buying 80%." Most of the purchased grapes come from Texas Hill Country vineyards, western Edwards Plateau vineyards near San Angelo, and the vineyards of Pecos County. As Fall Creek's newly planted vines come into fruition, the necessity for purchased fruit will not be as great. However, the Aulers plan to keep an aggressive grape purchase plan for Fall Creek to reduce the brunt of any future disasters and to continue to meet the strong demand for their wines which far outstrips supply each year. A 30% increase in production and sales was projected for 1995.

The newly planted acreage will contain Chardonnay, Sauvignon Blanc, Semillon, Emerald Riesling, Chenin Blanc, Cabernet Sauvignon, Merlot, Malbec, and Carnelian.

Another boon for Fall Creek was the addition to the staff in 1993 of Chad Auler, director of sales. His contributions are measurable. Sales jumped from 16,900 in 1994 to 22,000 cases in 1995. Production will increase in 1996.

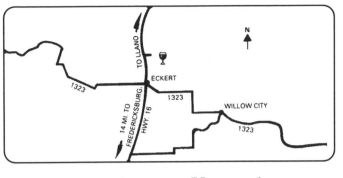

Bell Mountain Vineyards

Bob and Evelyn Oberhelman own and make wine at an estate winery in the Texas Hill Country.

BMV (formerly named Oberhellmann Vineyards, using the family's Old German spelling) is fourteen miles north of Fredericksburg, a town that was settled in 1846 largely by German immigrants. John Meusebach brought wagons loaded with 120 pioneers from New Braunfels to what was then the Indian frontier. To his credit, he made a lasting peace with the Comanches, something few were able to achieve.

Once settled, the Germans were a prodigious group. By 1847 they had constructed eighteen stores and the Nimitz Hotel. Its namesake was Chester Nimitz, a Texan of German ancestry who was promoted to commander of the Pacific fleet by President Franklin D. Roosevelt during World War II. His service was completed when he accepted the Japanese surrender aboard the USS *Missouri*. Nimitz was born in Fredericksburg, a grandson of the pioneer hotel man who also had boating interests, Capt. Charles Nimitz.

The German Texans have made many positive contributions to the state. By 1960 there were more than 400,000 persons with at least one-half German descent living in Texas, many of whom were doctors, engineers, and ranchers. Bob Oberhelman and his family are continuing the contributory tradition. The Dallas businessman now spends most of his time on Bell Mountain.

"On the slopes of Bell Mountain are vineyards and a

winery that we're dedicating to excellence," Oberhelman said. "It's reflected in our products and our facilities and certainly in the spirit of the people who take care of the vines and make the wine."

Oberhelman began to clear and prepare the fields for planting in 1974; the next year he built a farm house. In 1976, a trial vineyard was planted with twenty-four varieties, including both American and European selections. The trial period is described by Oberhelman:

> Later experiments with vinification helped in the choice of those varieties which would make superior wine. Each year we pulled up plants that couldn't measure up. At the end of the trial stage, the Old World premier grapes were favored. They endured and thrived in the Texas Hill Country climate. The soil, laden with mineral, clay, and gravel, was capable of making world-class wines.

Each year the vineyards have been expanded. The plants are from young vines which have been propagated in the Oberhelman nursery from special clones. According to Oberhelman,

> Wine is born in the vineyard. There are different tasks each season: pruning the plants during dormancy, fertilizing and cultivating in the early spring, spraying and training the vines during spring and summer, and harvesting in late summer. We give each task our devoted attention.

The plants are trained on a six-foot-high trellis system in order to permit maximum foliage development. Drip irrigation pipes allow a constant level of soil moisture for 725 plants per acre. Oberhelman says their efforts are directed toward the production of fine fruit.

> The grape variety is paramount in the consideration, and those grown in our vineyards are Chardonnay, Johannisberg Riesling, Gewurztraminer, Sauvignon Blanc, Semillon, Cabernet Sauvignon, Merlot, and Pinot Noir. At BMV, our winery develops and matures the wine. The process begins with crushing and destemming the fruit. At this point the white grapes are pressed immediately.

After separation from the skins and seeds, the juice travels through a cooling conduit for rapid chilling. It's inoculated with cultured yeasts and then fermented in refrigerated vats to encourage slow development at fifty to fifty-five degrees Fahrenheit.

Black grapes (also called red) are fermented on their skins to extract color and flavor. Pressing follows, and the wines are clarified during the winter. They are aged in either French Nevers oak puncheon barrels; American small, oak barrels; or stainless-steel tanks — depending on the style for the wine.

After the bulk aging period, the wine is bottled. Oberhelman said that since the wines are unpasteurized and contain no preservatives, they maintain scrupulous cleanliness. After bottling, the aging continues; for whites it is two to six months and for reds it is from six to twelve months.

Bell Mountain wines were twelve years in the planning before they were released. According to the winemaker, they knew from the earlier years of experimentation that they could make good wine. The grapes developed with the varietal character they were looking for and a balanced sugar-acid ratio that was needed. Winemaster Oberhelman is confident of continued success.

We have the technology to convert these grapes. We have recalled many well-wishers along the way. Foremost is Leon Adams, a friend and internationally known wine writer who visited us in August 1982. He sampled a full selection of our wines and said they had the potential to be "World Class." Of course, Leon was tasting experimental wines, but his words bolstered us. Then, almost two seasons later — May 1984 — our first wine was ready for the critical test. The wines were sound and well made, and we're confident that upcoming vintages will prove Leon right in his commentary.

The drought in 1984 made the vineyards dependent on the aquifer and four excellent property wells. After budbreak in late March, the vines received drip irrigation water twenty-four hours a day — 100,000 gallons per daily cycle. The dryness, however, practically eliminated disease. That

year also marked the first harvest for a two-acre block of
Cabernet Sauvignon and one acre of Semillon. In February,
6,200 Pinot Noir vines were planted, all certified Pommard
clones from the UC-Davis vineyards. Also that year, the winery was expanded to include room for empty bottle storage.
The year of the initial BMV offerings was 1984. There were
two labels: Bell Mountain Vineyards, a private reserve label
that identifies those wines grown, produced, and bottled on
the estate with varietal identification and vintage; and
Oberhof, premium wine produced and bottled at the winery
without grape identification, blend percentages, or vintage.

The 1985 vintage at Oberhellmann (now renamed
BMV) was reported excellent. The crop was well set with a
gradual maturation and favorable weather. Oberhelman
summarized the year:

> During July we cleared, graded, and root-plowed over
> thirty-three acres to the west of our Saint Joseph's Vine-
> yards. The soil is prime for vines — deep sandy loam, un-
> derlaid with sandstone and granite. The soil assay is high
> in iron and calcium oxide, which will yield rich and racy
> wines. We thinned the trees to the south and west of the
> future vineyard for good air drainage. Planting was com-
> pleted in St. Joseph's during the spring of 1986, and then
> we began planting the new vineyard.

Building construction on the property includes a truck
dock and glass warehouse. The Oberhelman residence,
Mariencrest — a Black Forest-style home that stands above
the Marienhof Vineyard — was finished in 1986.

> November 10, 1986, was a momentous day for the wine
> industry of Texas. It was then that the Department of
> Treasury, Bureau of Alcohol, Tobacco and Firearms, an-
> nounced the establishment of Bell Mountain Viticultural
> Area. It is the first Texas wine-growing appellation to be
> recognized by the federal regulatory agency. Bell Moun-
> tain will be dominant on our future labels with the logo
> bell as a trademark. It has the Lone Star in the center.
> The federal regulations are intended to name spe-
> cific areas which, due to unique soil conditions and ideal
> climate, can produce quality wines and therefore identify

and assure wine quality for the consumer. The Bell Mountain Viticultural Area, set at an elevation near 2,000 feet, has a moderate climate for fruit production. It has a warm but not too hot summer daytime temperature coupled with relatively mild cooler nights. The soils are distinctively high in minerals, notably iron oxide and typically high Hill Country calcium oxide. The area is on the slopes of Bell Mountain, highest peak in the region, which was first identified on the U.S. Geological Survey map of 1885.

We continue to expand our vineyards and now have fifty acres. The largest is in Cabernet Sauvignon — the Oberhellmann [BMV] 1985 Cabernet Sauvignon won numerous awards — next is Chardonnay, and the Pinot Noir. We'll produce modest amounts of Semillon, Gewurztraminer, Sauvignon Blanc and Riesling. Premium varietals is our direction. By 1988 we also had expanded the temperature-controlled cellars in order to age our bulk wine in barrels and our bottles. Since we do not release our white wines until they have been in the bottle up to a year and our red wines in excess of a year, additional space was demanded. All of our wines are estate bottled.

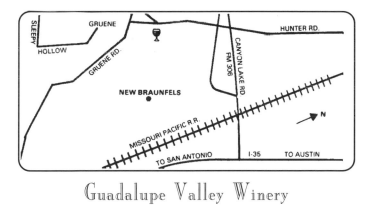

Guadalupe Valley Winery

German immigrants and Spanish *conquistadores* both have contributed viticultural interests to Texas. At the same time, many names for Texas features come from those who first settled the land. Comal County, for instance, took its name from the Comal River. It was named for a Spanish cooking utensil, a small earthenware pan used to prepare cakes made of maize. Apparently, the river had numerous little flat islands in it that reminded the Spanish of the pan.

The county is located on the Balcones Escarpment and was created from three other counties: Travis, named for the Alamo hero; Gonzales, an original county of the Texas Republic named for a one-time governor of Coahuila and Texas; and Bexar, named for the then ruling viceroy of the area.

The Comal feeds into the Guadalupe River, named by Capt. Alonso de Leon in 1689 in honor of the painting of the Lady of Guadalupe on his standard. The Spanish sent him to colonize Texas when they feared the French presence during the seventeenth century. He established the East Texas mission of San Francisco de los Tejas, one of several that failed and never was reestablished.

In Comal County near the Guadalupe River, the tiny town of Gruene (pronounced Green) is enjoying a reestablishment, the same sort of revitalization as the Texas wine industry. It was settled as early as 1850, but it wasn't until 1868 that H. D. Gruene began development there. He first constructed a general store. In 1900, he added a lumberyard, cotton gin, bank, and a beer and dancing hall, claimed to be the oldest in Texas. Gruene built a second cotton gin, and today it is the home of Guadalupe Valley Winery, the second winery to be bonded in Texas after Prohibition. Larry Lehr, the current winemaker, appreciates the winery's past.

> Today Gruene is reminiscent of days gone by. Merchants have worked hard to restore prosperity to the little community. Gruene, a German immigrant, accomplished wonders here. In just fifteen years he had established a number of businesses in what was referred to as "Schlaraffenland" (land of plenty), the name first given to the winery. He remained prosperous until the 1920s. Then a combination of drought, the boll weevil, and the Depression forced the family to sell the town.

At Gruene, now part of New Braunfels, the Guadalupe attracts tourists who enjoy riding down the river in tubes, canoes, or on rafts. They can rent the necessary equipment in town and then return after their water journey for a glass of Lehr's Guadalupe Valley wine at the old cotton gin. The strawberry or peach wines are novel refreshments after catching the rapids. Also available from the Villard Blanc, a French/American hybrid, or the Lenoir, an American variety, are white, red, and rose wines.

The winery was originally opened in 1975 as a cellaring and bottling operation, according to Lehr. He expounded:

> Wine was purchased in bulk from California and processed here. I bought it in 1980 with Dean Valentine, the winemaker here then. Now he's at Wimberley Valley.
>
> At the outset, only two wines were offered under the Schlaraffenland label — Hill Country White, made from 100 percent French Colombard, and Hill Country Rose, a blend of Ruby Cabernet, Barbera, Chenin Blanc, and Emerald Riesling. They were aged in American oak, which gave the wines an unusual complexity for their price, $2.00 a bottle.

Lehr wanted to use Texas grapes to make his wine, now renamed Guadalupe Valley. In 1976, he produced his first wine from all Texas grapes. It came from ten tons of French/American hybrids grown in Parker County. Lehr said the new rose was a blend of Chelois, Chancellor, and Chambourcin grapes — "grown, crushed, fermented, aged, and bottled in Texas."

"Since then we've produced several wines from grapes grown in Seguin, Crystal City, Del Rio, Bastrop, and Lubbock," he said.

Lehr's operation is a small one — approximately 600 cases a year. Most of it is sold to the tourists who come to discover Gruene or visit the river.

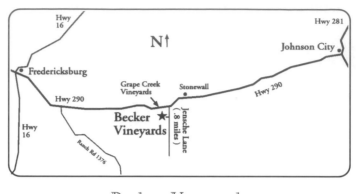

Becker Vineyards

Bunny and Richard Becker did such a thorough and delightful job of writing their stories for me that I've included both of them for your reading pleasure.

BECKER VINEYARDS, STONEWALL, TEXAS
By Bunny Becker

We bought the farm in 1990. Our plans were to buy an acre or two with an historic house to renovate, a place to go on weekends. Things didn't turn out that way. First, one- or two-acre farms are not let go by the area owners, especially family farms of historic interest, so we searched for a year or two and were lucky to find "the old Weber place." It consisted of a double pen cabin, one end of logs with the dog run filled in and a stone room attached, and numerous outbuildings, some log and some board and bat. It was on about 140 acres, part field and part natural area, fronting on Grape Creek.

As the property was land locked, only historic access from FM 1376 was available. This historic access was through three tracts of land settled in the 1850s, and still farmed by the descendants of the original settlers. It is said that this area along Grape Creek is the most intact historically for this reason. In the time of early settlement, families with adjoining tracts of land built their homes in the adjacent corners within "shouting distance" and "seeing distance" of each other for protection, and for the ladies, a bit of comfort at being able to see a neighbor. There were Indians nearby, and on the property, especially by the creek, numerous arrowheads have been found by our neighbors and ourselves. With the help of Johnny Ohlenberg of the Gillespie County Soil Conservation Agency, we have been able to plant native grasses and have contoured the land to prevent erosion.

The idea for a vineyard came from many sources. We have always had a large, too large, garden wherever we have lived. Also, we enjoy fine wine. And Richard is not afraid of hard work or taking on impossible tasks. After studying the county soil map and seeing and tasting the successes of our neighbors on Grape Creek, we decided to try planting grapes. My idea, of course, was to plant a test vineyard of one acre, and see how it did. Richard ordered a thirteen-acre test on an old field that had been let go to grass and mesquite. We found out from the owners that it had originally been farmed in peanuts. Now, with the most able assistance of our good friend, Armon Grantham, we have a test vineyard of thirty-six acres enclosed by deer fencing. Armon educated himself in planting and setting up a vineyard. Without him, we would not have been able to do it, as we live in San Antonio. Bob Miner was also a help in the construction, planting, trellising, and irrigation of the vineyards.

In March of 1993, the vineyard was ready. Our eldest son, Will, and his friends spent their spring break putting in trellis poles and wires just ahead of the planters. Armon planted the first grapes in the vineyards, and our youngest son, Joe, planted the last.

The following year we were joined on our project by Jim Brown and his family. He made our plans work. Jim and Armon put in the second vineyard, twelve acres, and we were joined by friends for planting as well as our children. Until Jim came, all of our weekends were spent doing chores in the vineyards, taping and spraying. We still do these things, but we know that Jim and his help will finish up. Jim works two jobs. He is an airplane mechanic and has taken viticulture courses at UC–Davis.

We were able to buy the adjoining (east) property, the old Peese place, in 1992. This made it possible to dream of our own winery as we now had access to a county road, Jenske Lane, connecting a mile down from U.S. Highway 290. The old Peese place contained around 150 acres and had a great horse pen and barn, plus an unrestored log cabin, the homestead of the Peese family. It is near this cabin, which we will restore as authentically as possible, that we will build our winery. We want the area to resemble an old homestead, cabin, barn, and windmill.

In 1994, we were delighted to have John Thomas, of Wildseed Farms, Inc., lease our fields and plant bluebonnets, purple horse mint, cosmos, and Indian blankets.

We have tried for several years to think of a proper name for our enterprise, but all of our best choices were already being used, and all the rivers, lakes, creeks, and mountains were taken. We wanted the name to be of the area, the place, or the people. Despite the contributions of family and friends (some quite artistic), nothing seemed to fit. So we will have to settle for a rather ordinary name and try to make extraordinary wine.

This year, as we build the winery, we are also putting in another vineyard, eleven acres, at the front of the property. Visitors will drive through this vineyard, the rows lined with yellow roses, through a field of bluebonnets to the winery, where in winter months they will be welcomed by a cheery fire in the barn containing the winery and tasting room. Our daughter, Clementine, will work in the tasting room. In other months, there will be a long porch for picnics and a historic cabin to explore.

DESCRIPTION OF THE WINERY AND VINEYARD
by Richard Becker

ACQUISITION OF THE FARM — Bunny and I had a long and shared dream of a Hill Country farm, not so much with vineyard and winery but a Texas place for two Texans, one from Abilene, me, and one from Texarkana, Bunny. We spent a number of years crisscrossing the Hill Country on farm to market roads; our favorite road became FM 1376, the road that heads north out of Boerne and was the old ox cart road for the immigrating Germans through the port of Indianola to the Prince Solms and ultimately Meusebach community of Fredericksburg. It's a road that passes through areas that remind us of Provence and that has re-minded others of the hills of Africa. The soil is a mix of limestone and in certain rare places, a deep sandy loam. Ulti-mately, the farm we found to buy was the old Weber place established in 1848 on Grape Creek. We loved the property. The house that we have refurbished as a headquarters was the twin pen dog run built by the German immigrants.

The soil is Heatly sand, which is a slightly acidic, deep sandy loam that has been the source of great success for the peach industry in the Hill Country. It occupies a fairly narrow band on both sides of the Pedernales between Fredericks-burg and a few miles east of Stonewall. The soil is interesting geologically. It contains upper layers of sand with underlying limestone, and pushing up through it all is what is called the Llano Uplift — Precambrian rock, which is rock that was ini-tially sediment in seas before there was any life on the planet, more than 500 million years old. These sediments ultimately sank and have pushed back up to the surface as granite in only a few places in the world, one of them being the Hill Country region around Stonewall and Johnson City.

We have a long interest in wine. The reason is not clear to either of us other than my wife's excellence as a French cook and my slow attempts to match wine with her food. We aspired to plant a vineyard by tasting wines produced in the Hill Country by our neighbors, Ned and Nell Simes, and subsequently by wines made by Ed and Susan Auler and Bob and Evelyn Oberhelman. The vineyard site was selected after consultation with Bob Oberhelman. He drove across our property on a hot August day, ultimately got out of the car and said, "If I were planting a vineyard, I would plant it here. This is the spot." Another day we searched with Enrique Ferro, our consultant from California, and after a day of digging in several sites and walking through corn fields and testing the soil with a spade, he said, "I would plant it here." We've planted vineyards in both the two separate spots selected by Bob and Enrique. The vineyard is 1,500 feet above sea level upon a slight rise above the Pedernales, perhaps at 100 to 150 feet, and what might be described as benchland. We planted Chardonnay in our thirty-six-acre vineyard as well as all the components of French Bordeaux, mainly Cabernet Sauvignon, but also Cabernet Franc, Malbec, Petit Verdot, and Merlot. I am interested in trying to find the right clones for our area, and accordingly, we have planted six clones of Chardonnay, including the two recently imported Dijon clones from France and six clones of Cabernet Sauvignon. I have been inspired by the clonal research done by Charles McKinney at the University of Texas Experimental Vineyard in Midland. Because of the similarities between our region and the Rhone Valley, including the soil, climate, the smell and look of the place, the scrub plants growing around, with the exception of cedar and mesquite, we are experimenting with Rhone varietals, including the first significant planting of Viognier in Texas, several thousand plants which will constitute a commercial effort to produce Viognier in this region, as well as planting approximately 250 plants each of Syrah, Mourvedre, Grenache, Roussanne, and Marsanne. We will ultimately be able to pick, crush, and vinify separately these other five varieties, age in French oak, and taste them to see what will come of this experimentation in the Texas Hill Country.

ESTABLISHING THE VINEYARD — No one can ever tell you how difficult or how costly this experiment will be. Five years ago, when we first became interested, we attended the Texas Grape Growers Association meeting in Lubbock, and while standing in a thirty-mile-an-hour wind in an experimental vineyard with Dr. Bill Lipe, I asked the vineyard manager from Llano Estacado what he guessed the cost of establishing a vineyard and winery would be. He turned around and looked at me and said, "Three million dollars." Bunny said I sank four feet into the High Plains soil and for that reason did not blow over. Certainly, it did not cost that much, but it is only because of the great help we have had from our neighbors and friends. The vineyard would never have been established without the appearance, deus ex machina, of Armon Grantham. Armon, a friend of several years, a career naval officer, born and raised on a farm in Mississippi, simply recognized that all the things to establish our vineyard would never be done without someone's help. My day job, which also involves most nights, didn't permit my constant presence on the vineyard site. Armon saw to the removal of the mesquite, erection of the deer fence, construction of the drip system, ripping with a bulldozer to a depth of four feet through the hard pan of many years of farming on our vineyard site, and overseeing many other aspects of planning. We were also helped initially by Bob Miner. Armon's son-in-law, Jim Brown, arrived to help plant vines in the first third of the vineyard. After three or four days of working with us, Jim said, "I think this is something I would like to do." Jim has continued as our vineyard manager. Jim is a mechanical genius and is responsible for the rebuilding of the old Weber homestead, repairing anything mechanical that doesn't work, and all subsequent plantings. We have now planted thirty-six acres, the last eleven of Sauvignon Blanc this spring. The first twelve acres will be in their third leaf this year (1995), and we will have our first crush.

DEVELOPMENT OF THE WINERY — In addition to the thirty-six acres of vineyard which are separated based on the soil strata which cross our land, we have four large fields which have been used for row crop production. At the end of our road, Jenske Lane, which crosses U.S. 290, John Thomas planted one of his first Hill Country flower fields in red poppies. It is a place of exceptional beauty in the Hill Country and has attracted great crowds. Bunny suggested that we talk to John about the possibility of using our corn fields as a place for wildflower seed production for his Wildseed Farms. A contract was completed two years ago, which has been nothing but a continuous pleasure for us and which includes separate (approximately forty acres) fields of bluebonnets, cosmos, purple horse mint, and a magnificent sixty-acre field of Indian blankets which surrounds the original homestead cabin built by the Webers in 1848. John harvests these fields for seed, separate from the wildflower center which he is planning for Highway 290, and is strictly for seed production. It has been a great source of delight for us. He said that the production from the Indian blanket field was the highest that he has had for that particular flower in Texas.

The winery has been constructed to include a cellar for our aging barrels. The cellar will run the length of the winery on one side and then turns and runs beneath the tasting room. We plan to make our wine in the French traditional method involving fermentation and aging in French oak, sur lie. The winery is constructed as a Hill Country barn with the tasting room in the front and the tanks set on the back for receiving grapes from the vineyards and separate rooms for bottling and storage. It is adjacent to the log cabin built in the 1850s by the Peese family, which is being refurbished. The site will resemble a nineteenth-century country farm scene with windmill, log structure, and barn. The entrance to the winery will be through the field of Sauvignon Blanc and to continue through a wildflower field to the vineyard. We planted yellow roses at the end of each row on the road through the vineyard, inspired by the plantings at Smith Haut Lafite in Bordeaux, which we visited with the Texas Wine and Grape Growers and Professor George Ray McEachern in November. The view from the winery front porch extends across the wildflower field to the eleven acres of Sauvignon Blanc and from the back of the winery across the field of bluebonnets to the twenty-five-acre vineyard of Cabernet Sauvignon, Viognier, and Chardonnay. The back vineyards are surrounded by a field of purple horse mint planted by John Thomas.

For someone who has worked hard to have a level of confidence in what the grape growers describe as his day job, the constant unanswerable questions and difficult to obtain answers are very frustrating. There are areas in the world where site selection is matched after long experience with clonal selection and rootstock selection as well as principles of watering, canopy management, and harvesting and vinification, and wine aging. None of those questions is answered for our place in the world, our microclimate, and our fruit. These questions must all be answered. The greatest challenge that I see is to begin addressing the issues of proper clonal selection, rootstock matching, watering principles, and the ways to grow our wine both in the vineyard and to age it properly in the winery. These questions will require many years and, I hope, many generations of our family in finding the answers.

The greatest pleasure for us has been the hard work that we have all done together, hard physical work under difficult conditions (it is always forty degrees and raining when we plant), the experiences of working with people as good as people can be (like Armon Grantham and Jim Brown), meeting our wonderful German neighbors who live up to the good things said about the German Hill Country people in every way and who have been nothing but helpful to us, and the oneness, the friendliness, the helpfulness of the other grape growers in the Hill Country, which has given us much heart, many times when we were feeling less than uplifted.

In rereading this, I realize that I sound as if we have already had a great success, which is not the case; we are only just beginning. But the experience of developing our place for grape growing and winemaking has been a very positive one for our family.

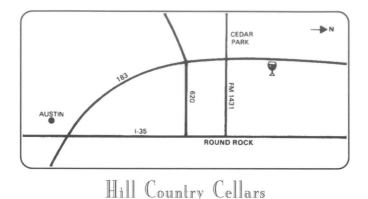

Hill Country Cellars

From his business perspective as a banker and real estate investor, together with a post prandial tradition of a fine cigar and Port, Fred Thomas was destined for the wine business. He had noted the awards being won by Texas vintners during the 1980s and became convinced that Texas soil could produce world-class wine.

Native Austinite Fred and his father, attorney Donald Thomas, intensely researched the Texas wine industry, agreeing on the need to establish the finest production facility with attention always to quality. The preferred location would be close to the Central Texas market, but it had to have climate and soil suitable for a vineyard. Hill Country Cellars' Cedar Park property was the answer to that search. Rather than razing the dilapidated, fifty-year-old ranch house on the site, originally built for a sheep operation, it was renovated and converted into a tasting room and winery office. The winery was constructed in a similar limestone, and the xeriscape of native plants completed the scheme to enhance and preserve the original property.

A focal point at the winery is the 200-year-old mustang grapevine. It was rescued (delighting residents who had made jelly from the grapes) from an old school site destined for a new gas station and moved to Hill Country Cellars to inaugurate the 1990 ground-breaking for the winery. It was quite a feat. The old vine, fifty-four inches in circumference, was entwined with a live oak tree. Specialists were called in for the task of excavating and moving by crane the 33,000-

pound composite. Placed next to a grove of centuries-old live oak trees, the area is used for picnics and festivals.

"The vine is a symbol of devotion to the land," Fred explained. "We hope that 200 years from now there will be a 400-year-old vine in Cedar Park."

Vineyards under the direction of then winemaker Penny Adams oversaw the planting of five acres of fifty rows containing 2,000 grapevines evenly distributed between Cabernet Sauvignon and Chardonnay in the spring of 1990. These *vinifera* vines are on their own rootstock, not grafted. Fruit is also bought from the state's many fine winegrowers. Antique rose bushes, used in the French tradition of indicator plants forewarning of fungal diseases, head each row.

Another Hill Country facility was used to produce the first vintage of Hill Country Cellars wines while the building of the winery was completed. The attractive label, primary-color arches on a black background, symbolizes the hills of the Texas Hill Country and won a national design award.

Hill Country Cellars hosts various activities: an annual grape stomp, the Texas Hill Country Wine and Food Festival, a Renaissance Festival, and musical and art events. The wines increasingly are garnering many awards.

Additionally, winemaker Russel Smith and cellarmaster Tom Gassone work to create and manage new programs: Hill Country Cellars' Brother Thomas sacramental wines, Don Thomas Fine Ruby Port, special labels, and (with the purchase in 1994 of Moyer Texas Champagne) plans to create a quality sparkling wine.

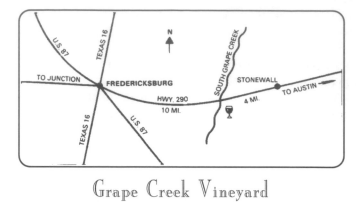

Grape Creek Vineyard

Ned Simes gives the Chilean government responsibility for his wine business.

"They were a major client of mine when I was in the offshore drilling business and I visited Chile five times a year," he said.

In 1966, Ned formed the Diamond M Company in Houston and expanded into Chile when friends requested a big jack-up rig to drill in the Straits of Magellan (where forty-two-foot tides change every six hours). He discovered the Chilean wines while working there and made everlasting friendships with people in the wine business. Then Allende took over the government and all the Americans left.

"My first work rule was that no one worked past age sixty-five," he said. "Guess who was the first one caught in that trap? Me."

Chilean friends offered Ned their expertise in locating the prime vineyard land at very favorable terms and conditions for him to remain in Chile. He wanted to go home, however, and transported the ideas to Texas.

"I read everything I could get my hands on about growing vines in the Texas Hill Country," he explained. "Nell and I spent every weekend of 1984 and 1985 looking at property."

Ned's criteria were acid soil, low rainfall but good ground water, windswept land without valleys, cool nights and warm days, and high visibility from a major U.S. highway. It took them a year and a half to find the property.

They prepared the first six acres in 1985 and hired a

horticulturist, planted the six acres in 1986, six more in 1987, four more in 1988, and made the first wine in 1989.

Ned and his son Leigh traveled the vineyards of Italy and Burgundy in 1989, and when they returned Leigh walked away from a fifteen-year medical practice, as well as interest in a hospital and a horse ranch, in order to come work with the family's Texas vineyard in 1990.

"This was a very prevalent area for grapes prior to Prohibition," Ned said. "At that time there were about twenty-six wineries throughout the state — quite a few in Gillespie County run by German immigrants."

The Simeses built the fermentation room in 1989 and the winery in 1990 and have been winning awards ever since.

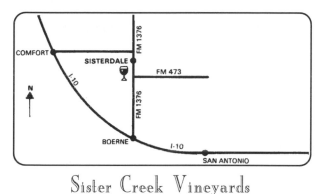

Sister Creek Vineyards

Sister Creek Vineyards is in the heart of the Texas Hill Country in Sisterdale (population twenty-five). Traditional French vines (Chardonnay, Pinot Noir, Cabernet Sauvignon, Cabernet Franc, and Merlot) are planted in the vineyard, located between cypress-lined East and West Sister Creeks. A century-old cotton gin has been restored to house the winery. French — especially Bordeaux and Burgundy — winemaking techniques are employed, including the aging of wine in French oak. There is minimal fining and filtering of the wine during the winemaking process in order to allow it to retain fullest flavors. Danny Hernandez, winemaker and vineyard manager, welcomes visitors by appointment during the week.

Spicewood Vineyards

Ed and Madeleine Manigold founded Spicewood Vineyards in 1990, shortly after they married. Ed had lived on a family farm as a youth, and this background led to his initial planting of a few vines on his property in Gonzales County. Madeleine's long-term commitment to live in the Texas Hill Country was instilled by her mother with visits to the family homestead in Burnet County.

After meeting, the Manigolds recognized a mutual love for fine wine, fine food, adventure, and the country life. Together they explored Napa and Sonoma Valleys, savoring the gold medal wines at the Sonoma County Fair. They vowed to find land in the Texas Hill Country, where they could grow wine grapes and make high quality Texas wines.

Fortunately, the Manigolds found excellent land thirty-five miles from Austin off Highway 71 in Spicewood, Burnet County. It took two years to build a cabin, locate the much needed and precious water, and to learn about growing grapes and making wine. They traveled to conventions of the American Society of Enology and Viticulture, took courses at the University of California at Davis, studied at Grayson County Community College with Dr. Roy Mitchell, developed pruning skills under the tutelage of Dr. Charles McKinney and Carolyn and Frank Carpenter at the University of Texas System Experimental Vineyard, and studied wine sensory evaluation with Sarah Jane English. A trip to Bordeaux with Dr. George Ray McEachern instructed the Manigolds about French viticultural and enological practices. And as if that were not enough, they joined the Texas Wine and Grape Growers Association, the Texas Hill Country Wine Guild, and the Texas Hill Country Wine and Food Festival Board of Directors to share experiences and learn from other pioneers in the wine grape industry.

With this growing knowledge, the Manigolds planted their first acre in 1992, including Merlot (Ed's favorite), Cabernet Sauvignon, Chardonnay, Sauvignon Blanc, and Riesling. They expanded to five acres in 1993 and ten in 1994. To the initial varieties they added small amounts of

Zinfandel, Muscat, and Cabernet Franc. Six more acres were scheduled for planting in 1996, with a maximum capacity of thirty acres on the present site.

Spicewood Vineyards is located in an ancient river bed on the edge of the Llano Uplift. In looking for water they found a fault running through the property with a displacement of more than 400 feet. The soil has tremendous complexity, ranging from Trinity sands to red, loamy clay. The vineyard slopes downward from an elevation of 900 feet and benefits from strong, southeasterly breezes that provide excellent ventilation. To maximize the conversion of Texas sun into quality wine, the Manigolds are using a vertical-shoot positioning trellis and close plant spacing to control vigor.

In 1993 construction began on a small winery that will be used for five years. Plans are in process to build a larger winery before the turn of the century.

At the present time the Manigolds are planting a small demonstration vineyard called "Grapes Over Texas." It features viticultural practices from counties that have contributed to the development of the Texas wine grape industry. Visitors may tour the world of grape growing right in the heart of the Texas Hill Country.

4

North Central and Eastern Texas Vineyards

There are two reasons for drinking wine . . . when you are thirsty,
to cure it; the other, when you are not thirsty, to prevent it . . .
prevention is better than cure.
— Thomas Love Peacock, *Melincour*

The Cross Timbers, Blackland Prairie, Grand Prairie, and Post Oak Belt are important geographical designations for north central Texas. They merge in gentle, gregarious ways rather than expressing the landscape by stark interruptions. No one can be certain just how distinct the regions were thousands of years ago, but man changes land by using it just as the elements of weather alter and reshape it. Between man and nature, today this section of Texas has treeless expanses, savannas, and grasslands that brush against strips of avocado and bottle green forests. The Cross Timbers, more readily identified in the last century, represents two parallel woodlands that stretch from north to south through the plains and prairies and their changing landscape.

Sometimes the land is flat. At the next moment it may jut up into a mesa, or become rolling plains, or down the road incline into a series of slowly rising hills. It is an immense area covering approximately 67,000 of Texas' total 267,339 square miles.

The Red River, the northern border, is no longer entirely the color that once named it. After the red muddy water is cleansed by Lake Texoma, it is diamond blue-white, clear as Baccarat. It and the other river systems — Brazos, Colorado, and Trinity — help create the prosperous vineyards, farmland and ranches, furnishing the luscious largesse of handsome cattle, rich foodstuffs, and shimmering cotton.

There is, however, red soil, a product of a geological time when the rocks consisted largely of sandstone and shale. This was the period when the amphibians declined and the reptiles increased. In Texas, dinosaurs tracked through some of the river beds and left their footprints.

At other places the land is black, mysteriously black, a change that occurs when limestone dissolves into dirt. Waxy and fertile, it is filled with nutrients, pregnant with production that comes from calcareous chalk for wild plums and grapevines. Blackland Prairie is nature's most bounteous Texas grassland. An old-timer once said: "Man lives on grass and water," not literally, of course, but by eating the beef that graze on grass, drinking the milk that cows have converted from grass, bread crops, and so forth.

Wooded areas range from plentiful cedars to scrawny blackjack or lush post oak. Some trees have branches that reach across to one another, forming an unceasing airy network for squirrels who race along hurriedly and pause nervously to flip their tails and fuss. Trees often are distances apart, too — a solitary hackberry or scrubby mesquite crops up only sporadically.

The land is as diverse as its size — mountain ranges with gaps that used to let wagon trains or herds of buffalo pass through, gates for the ever-roaming Comanches and a thoroughfare for the cattle drives; black dirt; red earth; white hills and green forests; farm and ranch land; plains and prairies.

Parker County, situated on both the Grand Prairie and the Cross Timbers, is strictly Texan. No Spanish settlement ever located there, nor did early Americans establish themselves in the area. It wasn't until 1849 that the county received its first permanent settlers. With an annual mean temperature of sixty-four degrees, rainfall that averages thirty-one inches a year, and an altitude of 900 feet, the land

was ideal for grazing cattle and raising horses. Horses, however, attracted Indians. The Indians raided so repeatedly
that a leading Indian fighter of the day published a newspaper called *Whiteman* to inform settlers against the savages
and encourage self-protection. In any event, the settlers
stayed, farmed, ranched, and developed the country.

Throughout its history, Parker County has earned
eighty percent of its income from beef, hogs, dairy cattle,
hay, peanuts, melons, and peaches. But there's a newcomer.
Today the agribusiness of that region includes grapes that
make Parker County wine. There were three wineries, La
Buena Vida, Château Montgolfier, and Sanchez Creek. Now
only one remains.

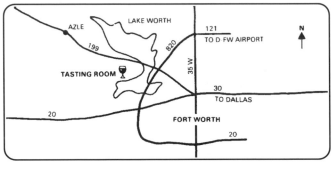

La Buena Vida Vineyards

"We're in the middle of a wine revolution in Texas,"
said Dr. Bobby Gene Smith, an Arlington osteopath and
founder of La Buena Vida Vineyards (LBV) in Parker
County. "We know which grapes do well in this climate and
we know how to process them. We have the technology, too,
so all we need is time to reach full potential. This is only the
beginning."

Smith, a twentieth-century pioneer in the Texas wine
industry, planted the first *Vitis vinifera* and French/Ameri-
can hybrid vines in the area in 1974. He produced his initial
wine four years later — 1,500 gallons. If the endeavor sounds
easy, it wasn't. He searched several years before he found
just the right sort of land: gentle slopes with small valleys for

proper drainage, a prevailing southwesterly breeze to help
cool the summer heat, sandy clay soil, about twenty-seven
inches of rain a year, and an abundance of peach trees
nearby. He described the beginnings:

> André Tchelistcheff, the renowned California vintner
> [who died in 1994] told me to look for land with lots of
> native grapes and peaches. The native, wild grapevines
> grow all over the place here, and Parker County is the
> peach capital of Texas. As it turned out, *finding* the land
> was the easy part. Making the vineyards liked to have
> killed me. I used to spend the weekends out here,
> sleeping in my pickup next to the old metal barn. I could
> hear the armadillos and possums rooting around, but af-
> ter a day of working in the fields, they didn't keep me
> awake.

Smith used to work his father's vineyards in Alabama
where he was reared, the youngest of six children. His
special job was to tend to the grape arbor. They sold the
muscadine to local merchants and jelly producers. The
strongly Southern Baptist family made no alcoholic beverages, of course. Smith didn't have his first taste of wine
until he was eighteen years old and in the Air Force. He
served in the medical corps at Sheppard Air Force Base in
Wichita Falls, Texas. His introduction to the Lone Star state
was compelling, and he decided to stay to practice here.

The doctor-turned-winemaker is as friendly as a hound
pup, and he hasn't lost his slow, soft, southern approach to
words. Don't be misled, however. His soft speech has tenac-
ity when it comes to the wine business.

For example, in 1976 he spoke often and convincingly
for state legislation that allowed growers to make wine in
dry Parker County. The result was the Farm Winery Act of
1977, which permitted the viticulturists to produce and
bottle wine in dry counties as long as distribution occurred
outside them.

There have been other notable firsts, too. A product of
LBV's first wine year, the 1978 Rayon d'Or, received a gold
medal and "best of its class" in the Eastern U.S. Wine

Competition of 1979. There were 630 wines entered. Rayon d'Or won another gold medal in 1980.

La Buena Vida is continuing to produce quality wines in Texas, where wine has been made since 1662 – 100 years before wine grapes were grown in California. In 1984, LBV was the second Texas winery to produce sparkling wine, releasing its first bottles of Blanc de Noirs. Not bad when you consider that the winery made its first commercial wines just six years before that, and in milk tanks converted to wine vats, no less. Nonetheless, some of those vines are now older and capable of producing more mature, fuller flavored grapes. Bobby's enthusiasm about the winery is clear:

> This has been a dream of mine for some time. Our family has worked hard to produce quality *cuvées* (blended wines) made exclusively from Texas-grown grapes. Our grapes possess all the essential characteristics necessary to produce sparkling wines, such as low pH, high natural acidity, and ideal sugar content. In late 1985 we released 400 cases of Blanc de Blancs Natural, Brut, and Sec – all made by the *méthode champenoise*.

Now Smith's son Steve makes the wine, and according to him, the wine business is part of the bonding of their family.

> I believe our name, Buena Vida, says it all. It means "the good life." That's what we want our wine to create. I want to involve my children in it – the way we've been involved – and leave it to them. Give them a wine opportunity.

Steve believes that Parker County is developing and will continue to develop as one of the better wine-producing regions in Texas. He said they are beginning to have enough time and experience behind them to prove it.

The Smiths built the visitor's center because they like to be close to their customers and they want to sell their own wine. Steve thinks they are successful as a regional winery that produces wines with a regional character.

In 1994 Smith bought an old church on two acres of land in historical downtown Grapevine, and it has been remodeled for the La Buena Vida tasting room. The adjacent garden is filled with native plants, herbs, arbors, and a show vineyard. Visitors are invited to enjoy wine and cheese or a picnic in the lovely area.

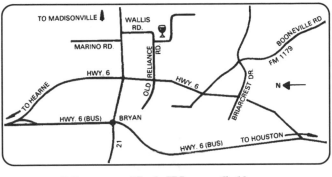

Messina Hof Wine Cellars

History records that probably the first Italian to see Texas was Amerigo Vespucci in 1497. In the nineteenth century, two Italian soldiers fought on opposite sides in the war for Texas independence: Prospero Bernardi with the Texans at San Jacinto, while Vicente Filisola was Santa Anna's second in command. Now the Bonarrigos are producing Texas wines where some of the first Italians settled. According to Merrill Bonarrigo, general manager of Messina Hof Wine Cellars in Bryan, immigrants brought grapevines from the old country to plant in the Brazos Valley.

> They also brought the rich traditions of grape growing and winemaking. The land at the site of Messina Hof was originally planted in cotton and watermelons by the Rizzo and Cangelose families. Wild grapevines were abundant. Today the land is planted in *vinifera* and pine trees.

In the wine industry, tradition is the rule, not the exception, and Messina Hof is a perfect example. It is among the rising stars of Texas' wineries, and vintner Paul Bonarrigo (bow-nuh-ree-go) brings a lot of Old World family know-how to his winemaking. The heritage and his given name go back more generations than he can remember.

"In my family, the first son is always named Paul," he said. "When he reaches age fifteen, his responsibility for making the family wine begins."

For this Paul Bonarrigo that event happened in the Bronx, New York, in 1961. His grandfather Paul brought the family to "Little Italy" in 1927, and his father Paul stayed and reared his family there. In that section of New York, all the families were from Sicily. They had come to this country to find a better way of life, but they brought their traditions with them — one of which was winemaking.

> Grandfather had a vineyard and winery in Messina, but the tradition of Italian winemaking in the United States had to begin on a much smaller scale. They didn't have the land to plant vineyards. Grandmother would send her sister to the produce market with the exact kind and amount of grapes to buy. Then we'd make the wine in the basement.

The family saved winemaking for the weekends. Grapes were stacked in boxes along the floor. Several varieties were needed to suit his grandmother's blend. Bonarrigo remembers that the whole clan — aunts, uncles, cousins, sisters, and brothers — would take turns with the nineteenth-century, hand-cranked, wooden press.

> It held forty pounds of grapes. That amount makes about three gallons of wine. The legal limit for a family's quota of wine was 200 gallons, and it took many, many pressings of the grapes. I don't know exactly how much we produced but we were never short of wine.

Although Paul's grandfather made additional wine to sell to the people of his village in Italy, the commercial aspect ended when he moved to New York. The Messina Hof vintner is the first Bonarrigo to make and sell wine in the United States. To mark the beginning of this tradition, he produced Papa Paulo Porto, a Texas port that pictures the passing of knowledge from one generation to the next on the label.

"Someday my son, Paul Mitchell Bonarrigo, will join us in the winemaking business," he said.

A physical therapist by profession, Bonarrigo served a tour of duty for the U.S. Navy in California at the Oakland Naval Hospital. During that time he became familiar with the Napa Valley wineries and even took courses at the Napa Wine School. He was extremely impressed:

> These were some of the grapes my family had used to make our wine. I appreciated what was happening in Napa and took some courses at University of California at Davis. It gave me a modernistic viewpoint of what my grandmother had been trying to do. What she had taught me through the senses, UC-Davis was teaching with technology. My grandmother had talked about tartness and sweetness and what she had discussed basically was acidity and sugar in the wine.

A Texan befriended Bonarrigo in Florida at a physical therapists' meeting and encouraged him to practice in the Lone Star state. He recommended Bryan especially.

"I had attended Bryan Elementary School in the Bronx, and his suggestion was so ironic it almost seemed like a sign," Bonarrigo said. "So I moved to Bryan, Texas, and met my wife."

Merrill Bonarrigo is a native of Bryan. Her heritage is German and her ancestors lived in Hof, hence the name of the wine honors both families — Messina Hof.

The Bonarrigos had planned to build a small, 1,000-gallon winery, just enough to fulfill the federal requirements for commercial production. But after their first harvest, they received multiple telephone calls from local growers who had no market for their grapes. Merrill described what ensued:

> We added a room onto the winery in one week. We converted a shed into a fermenting area, and that made our capacity almost 9,000 gallons.

When Paul bought his used 1949 Ford tractor he'd never been on one, and he had several close calls trying to master how to use it. Eventually, the land was prepared and the Bonarrigos planted every vine on their one-fourth-acre test plot themselves. Once the labor of love was completed, Merrill carefully photographed each row. Paul at first thought it humorous.

> I asked her why she had bothered. All eleven pictures looked identical, just little sticks set into the ground. But she was right. Each row was marked with the grape variety, and we've used the photos as part of our tour at Messina Hof to show the beginning and progress of our vineyard.

In preparation for their larger operation, the Bonarrigos bought a historic piece of property that was moved to Messina Hof. It's not the first time the building has been moved. In 1901, it was transported from Galveston to become a private school for girls, Villa Maria Ursuline Academy. Then it was the home of the ambassador to Great Britain during World War I, Will Howell. He changed the Victorian Gothic style to a French country home, and it is now an attractive addition to the Messina Hof winery.

Messina Hof wines have been awarded many gold, silver, and bronze medals during the past several years, and Paul plans to keep on garnering medals for his prize-winning wines.

From its humble roots, Messina Hof has emerged as the most awarded and fastest growing Texas wine. By mid-1994, it had already won "Best of Texas" at the Houston Club competitions for an unprecedented three consecutive years — twice for its Cabernets and once for its Papa Paulo Private Reserve Port. Year after year, Messina Hof continues to win the most awards in the Texas Restaurant Association's "Texas Wine Classic" and the Texas Department of Agriculture's "Lone Star State Wine Competition," including the Star of Texas Grand Award in 1993.

But the wine's recognition isn't confined within state lines. In 1994, it became the first Texas wine in ten years to earn a double gold medal at the Tasters Guild International Wine Judging in Fort Lauderdale, Florida. *The Wine Spectator* rated its "Angel" Late Harvest Johannisberg Riesling a "90" on a 100-point scale in 1992, ranking it the Best Regional Wine.

Messina Hof's Chenin Blanc and Johannisberg Riesling have both been served at the White House, and former first lady Barbara Bush rates the Johannisberg Riesling among her favorites. Owners of the highly-esteemed Star Canyon restaurant in Dallas and the Oxford Street Restaurant and Pub chain in Texas and Louisiana both chose Messina Hof for their private house wines.

The physical winery has also made quite a mark for itself. In 1993 alone, 70,000 visitors from all over the world toured Messina Hof — quite a feat for a community of 100,000 people. Hundreds of people descend upon the grounds for four weekends in the summer to harvest the vineyards' grapes, and other festivals and outdoor events maintain Messina Hof's status as the state's most visited winery.

Bonarrigo blends all his varietal grapes because he doesn't believe in a pure presentation. The federal requirement for a varietal states that it must contain seventy-five percent of the variety named on the bottle, so that leaves the winemaker twenty-five percent leeway to develop his or her style for the wine.

"All my white wines will have a very nice acid balance because I like that acid finish," Bonarrigo said. "I want to present a wine that has good acid to sugar balance, a sharp, distinct flavor with vigor and energy."

The winemaker does make a difference. One year the University of Texas gave its Chenin Blanc grapes to four Texas winemakers for them to make wine. The grapes were harvested the same day, off the same row of vines of exactly the same Chenin Blanc.

"Each of those wines was totally different," Merrill said. "It was incredible how distinctive each one was."

At Messina Hof the Chenin Blanc is unusually full-bodied. According to Bonarrigo, the grape is suitable for a variety of treatments — everything from bone dry to a dessert wine. The 1983 vintage set the style. He harvested the crop on July 22 and fermented the juice through August 8 at fifty-eight degrees. It was filtered and bottled on November 11, and the chemistry at bottling time was pH 3.35, semi-dry finish with the alcohol eleven percent by volume.

Bonarrigo described a product of that successful year:

> We made the first jeroboam ever filled in Texas. There
> were only ten, and we sold every one of them the first
> week they were available — our 1983 Texas Cabernet.

The 1984 and 1985 vintages came from grapes planted
in 1980. That was a particularly remarkable year for the
Bonarrigos. Merrill explained:

> We planted an additional eight acres in 1980. There was
> an incredible thing that happened that year. We had pur-
> chased the stock, we had it and the land prepared and
> ready, and on the day we were to plant, it snowed. So we
> call vineyard two our snow vineyard. It didn't stop us. We
> planted the entire eight acres, and it was thirty-four
> degrees. Until we expanded the vineyard to thirty acres,
> only Paul and I worked the land.

The Messina Hof vintner likes to make his red wines in
a Bordeaux style. His plan is to always present premier
wines from the best quality grapes he can grow.

> Basically, my style of winemaking reflects the kind of wine
> I personally prefer. For whites, I admire the German style
> and my Late Harvest Riesling and Vina di Amore Sweet
> Bianco resemble that style. For reds, it's Bordeaux — rich
> in tannin, excellent staying power, fruity but also deep in
> color with a lovely oak flavor.

Bonarrigo says his name means good (*bona*) king (*rigo*).
Hof is the German word for chateau or palace. Merrill and
Paul believe there's a significance to the names in their heritage, and they intend to continue the traditions that have
always been important to the family. They aim to make
wines fit for a king and preserve the history in a unique winery that expresses what Messina Hof represents.

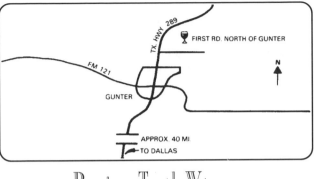

Preston Trail Winery

Preston Trail Winery is named for one of the most widely used roads during the development of Texas commerce. It began in 1839 when Albert Sidney Johnston, secretary of war for the Republic of Texas, planned a series of forts along the frontier. He commissioned William Cooke to lay out a military route from Austin to Coffee's Station, established two years earlier when Holland Coffee built his trading house on the Red River. Sam Houston established Fort Preston at Coffee's Station and named it for the commanding officer, according to *The Handbook of Texas.* (Preston was also the name of Johnston's first wife.)

Preston became an extremely important point of entry and port. Everything was imported. Texas was populated mostly by farmers who seldom produced enough for their families, much less have extra to sell. Consequently, the river traffic was strategic, even though the river was seasonal and unreliable. Later, Preston Trail was incorporated among the great cattle drives, and today Dallas' Preston Road is a transportation route to Preston Trail Winery.

The winery is owned by Don and Ruby Prescott and Tiffany and Tom Greaves. Greaves is the vineyard manager and winemaker. When he graduated from New York University with a master's degree in nuclear engineering, his wife gave him a winemaking kit to celebrate the occasion. Tom Greaves explained:

> What we have here is a hobby that's gotten out of hand.
> I've made wine out of every kind of vegetable or fruit. I've

made wine out of potatoes, at Thanksgiving it was cranberries. I made a list once and there were over 100 vegetables and fruits that I've made wine from. At one time there were twenty names under A, beginning with apple, apricot, and anise. My Bible in the early days was folk wine — apple champagne, almond wine, banana, barley, several berries — boysen, current, goose, dew. Finally, I planted my own berries.

Greaves was a computer programmer for IBM. As such, he frequently moved, and on one such occasion (from 1974 to 1980) lived in California. The family had a large home with a lot of yard. He replanted the backyard to a vineyard and converted a bedroom to the winery.

I bought Cabernet Sauvignon grapes from Nathan Fay in the Stag's Leap area in Napa Valley. I grew 150 vines and each vine made a gallon of wine. I'd buy wine for drinking and give away the wine I made. I still prefer to buy to keep current on the most important wines of the day. Then I discovered oak aging. I even put the barrels in the bedroom — just having a ball and loving to make wine. I knew I'd found my retirement career. I researched wine fields and discovered Texas. When I was up for transfer again, I requested Texas so I could start my vineyard. That's how we got here. We moved to Dallas in June 1980.

Greaves said it took him one hour to find and buy his home, but he searched for vineyard land for months. Finally, he found a hill he liked in Gunter, Texas, north of Dallas. There was a mobile home on the property so he could stay there on the weekends and be back in Dallas for the week.

Our first vines were from Oberhellmann Vineyards (now Bell Mountain Vineyards, near Fredericksburg), rootings on their own roots. Seyval Blanc was the only hybrid I bought. The others were French Colombard, Chardonnay and in the next year I ordered *vinifera* grafted onto dogridge. It was recommended by Texas A&M, but dogridge is very difficult to graft onto and nearly all the cuttings have been unproductive. Bench graftings on

dogridge have to be precise — less than one percent survive while the normal rate is 98 percent.

At this point, Greaves' experiences began to read like
the book of Job. He started scouring the country for other
plants and found a California producer who had had a can-
cellation from a Napa grower, so he bought his order. There
were over 3,000 vines, but only five or six survived because
they were planted in the dead of winter without irrigation.
He explained:

> That summer, 1982, we were nursing along the Oberhell-
> mann plants. I decided I didn't need drip irrigation. If the
> vines would last for two or three years, they'd be drought-
> resistant because the roots would be deep enough. So I
> bought a 600-gallon fertilizer tank that my son and I
> pulled through the vineyard on a tractor. When our fam-
> ily left for a vacation for a week in mid-July, the vines were
> gorgeous and thriving. I had planted 1,800 vines. When
> we returned, nearly 1,200 were dead from water stress.
> My son and I got out the tank and tractor. It took us an
> hour to fill it with water. Then the tractor wasn't big
> enough to pull it up the hill, so I emptied out half the
> water and we pulled the tank. It took three days to water
> the vineyard, and the plants needed more than we could
> give them. I decided to pick out the healthiest vines on
> the lowest part of the hill and we kept watering them. The
> rest died.

By 1983, only 600 of the initial 5,000 plants were alive.
That year he planted another 5,000 vines, Cabernet Sauvignon and some other *vinifera* varietals. This time, however, he had an irrigation system installed.

> At this point I had lost $300,000 and gained only $500. It
> was a terrible learning experience. Nor did we realize
> how difficult it was to keep weeds down and to spray the
> area (nine acres) for fungus and other things. A weed
> badger — it equals seventy people with a hoe — can cover
> two acres a day, but I only had two days, the weekend, to
> work it. And the plants had to be sprayed every week
> against black rot and oidium.

Greaves replanted, expanded, and built a small winery in 1984. The nine acres of new vines had to be staked and trained, a task that he estimated would take ten minutes per vine. With 5,000 new vines, that came to 1,000 hours a week. He also found time to complete the wooden frame structure for the winery; however, a wind storm destroyed it during construction and another one had to be built.

> Once again I had to cut my expenses and select which vines to save. This time I had some help from local kids. It took 1984 and 1985 to get the vines on wires. By this time I had a sprayer, pre-emergence herbicide (sprayed by hand), and the weeds were now under control. The vines were trained on the stakes and 1986 was going to be the first big year. There was great vigor and the vines had huge growth, at least four to six feet. I just knew that this had to be our year, at last. Then the hail storm came on April 19, 1986. It lasted one hour. I walked out into the vineyard after that and every cane on every vine was broken off at the base at the ground. All the new growth was ruined. All the clusters, everything was gone. My heart was broken. There was nothing left.

It took more than three weeks for Greaves to gain enough courage to go back to the vineyard. When he did return, the vines had started recovering and ended up producing almost three tons per acre (ten had been expected). The quality had extraordinary statistics: brix 22.2, pH 3.2 and 3.4, total acidity 0.9 or higher on every variety. He said the grapes produced excellent wine, so he and his partner, Don Prescott, bonded the winery in July 1986.

Greaves' vineyard is forty miles north of Dallas near Gunter. Prescott has an eight-acre vineyard ten miles from Greaves, where he grows Sauvignon Blanc and Cabernet Sauvignon on Champanel, exclusively. Their first production, 1986, was 1,300 gallons—half of it from Charles Britt's vineyard, ten acres in Collinsville.

They felt certain that 1987 was going to be their year, but a freeze on March 29 caught the vines with their leaves out. The expected twenty tons at Greaves' vineyards became five tons.

Preston Trail's 1987 Merlot Blanc won "Best of Show" award at the Grapevine Texas Wine Competition. The 1987 French Colombard won a gold medal at the Southwestern Wine Competition in Santa Fe, and Tiffany (a slightly sweet white wine) and the Chenin Blanc won bronzes. Preston Trail also produces Cabernet Sauvignon and White Burgundy, a total of 1,800 gallons in 1987, and about 4,000 gallons in 1988.

At the time of updating *The Wines of Texas* in 1995, alternative operations were being considered by the owners.

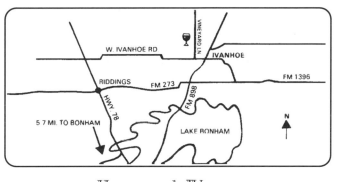

Homestead Winery

Barb and Gabe Parker started their wine journey in the early 1980s. Business trips to the California wine country and experimenting with some home winemaking created an insatiable interest. They acknowledged the patience, time, and energy it takes to develop a first-rate vineyard, dug in their heels and their shovels, and went to work.

Gabe's family had farmed in Ivanhoe for more than 100 years, so soil, pests, weather, and various vicissitudes were no mystery. The renewal of grape growing in Texas ignited the action that led the Parkers to plant a vineyard in 1983. They tried several varietals — Cabernet Sauvignon, Zinfandel, and Chenin Blanc — proving that grapes were a viable North Texas crop and establishing themselves as the local source for techniques and general know-how.

Research continues on several other possible varietals with a number of growing techniques under evaluation. The main vineyard of Cabernet Sauvignon is now more than ten years old and in its prime. Five more acres have been added to satisfy the need for grape production. Still, the Parkers need to purchase grapes from other local growers with their same high standards to satisfy the demand for their products.

"Wine quality starts in the vineyard," Gabe explained. "Our winery is a natural outgrowth of our vineyard efforts."

The Parkers took a deliberate approach to learning as they put together their operation. It took four years to build the winery building, a project of Gabe and his many friends. The name Homestead Winery was selected because the property location is the Parker homestead. Quality winery equipment was purchased and cost was a major consideration. The idea was to permit the Parkers to produce a reasonably priced product.

"We believe that wine should be priced so it can be enjoyed every day," Gabe said.

According to the Parkers, the final ingredient for success was the winemaker. Their answer was Mike Vorauer, who spent ten years plus in the Texas wine industry before coming to Homestead. The Parkers believe that his dedication to the art and his concern for quality can be tasted in each glass of wine.

"His knowledge of Texas fruit and the necessary winemaking techniques to create great wines is unmatched," Gabe said.

Homestead wines have received much recognition and have won numerous awards.

5

Wine Country of the High Plains and Western Texas

Wine is the intellectual part of the meal;
meats are merely the material part.
— Alexander Dumas

Regions of Texas have similar features, of course: rivers, plains, hills, and so forth. Nonetheless, regional character emphasizes the distinctions that separate one section from another. In northern Texas, for example, the verdant or wheat-colored prairies, forests, and boundless plains dominate. The distinguishable Texas Hill Country is laced with natural springs, limestone hills, and lakes. West Texas has vast vistas, plateaus, basins, and mountains. Some portions of the lands seem friendlier, almost beckoning in invitations to come explore; consequently, visitors do come, making annual treks that form trails as seasonally reliable as the settler and buffalo routes of earlier times. The Trans-Pecos, however, appears mostly exempt from sojourners who return with circadian persistence. It is the most untouched part of Texas, attracting mellowed stoics whose special brand of enchantment can conjure fairylands from deserts.

There's a memorable solitariness in the Trans-Pecos. Independent mountain ranges divide themselves from one another with erosive materials they have deposited for centuries to create land distance between them. Caliche and creosote bushes have claimed these mountain-made low-

87

lands. The mountains, however, are part of the earth's crust, fractures jutting upward like a slightly filled bellows on one side but sharply declining on the other. Coolness, being a brazen stranger in this dry, waterless Southwest, does find some expression among the taller peaks. The Trans-Pecos has the highest elevation and greatest diversity of geology in the state. And Big Bend National Park is the only place in the United States where the Rocky Mountain and Appalachian Mountain systems visibly converge. One range called the Chisos frequently has ghostly cloud apparitions hovering near the summits; hence, some say Chisos means "ghost." Another popular legend credits the name to the last chief of the local Apaches. He and his squaw, it is said, returned to their native mountain to die after escaping their white captors. Their cloudlike ghosts remain.

The mountain forests of oak, pine, juniper, and fir contain flora and fauna that are found no other place in the United States. Another range, the Guadalupe Mountains, houses the finest fossil repository in the world. Here also are located the ephemeral water courses that eschew the rest of this country. Many biologists and geologists consider the Trans-Pecos a paradise. Nevertheless, it is different from the other Trans-Pecos areas just as the Trans-Pecos is different from the rest of Texas. The deserts are there, all right—dry, forbidding, durable and intense, dotted with bright red cactus flowers and their soft green thorny blades. But the Trans-Pecos is a place of strong contrasts: virile forests, wildflower-filled mountains, salt flats, barren rockscapes, canyons, plains and plateaus, and the narrow, fertile Rio Grande Valley where the river carved its way through the mountains.

Vineyards in the Trans-Pecos have been at its extremities—El Paso, Fort Stockton, Del Rio—and verge on adjacent regions, the High Plains, and the Edwards Plateau.

The limestone base of the Edwards Plateau travels thousands of feet toward the center of the earth. Grasslands and savannas cover it to satisfy the livestock that give the place its major living, the most outstanding grazing region in Texas. The rich limestone soils that developed in the Blackland Prairie failed to materialize here for lack of rain. But water trapped in the limestone formations provides this section of Texas some of the clearest, freshest, and most abundant spring-fed streams imaginable. The Edwards Plateau is the southernmost unit of the Great Plains — those waving grasslands that extend from Canada to Texas, a memorable phenomenon.

One rather unmemorable stream, the Pecos River, unites or divides the Edwards Plateau, the Trans-Pecos, and the High Plains, the big three of West Texas.

The High Plains progresses by a series of long cliffs with intervening expanses of more level ground called escarpments. There are basins as well. The natural vegetation is short grass; in fact, this area was once a leading grazing land. It is still one of the most distinctive short grass regions in the United States, but the properties of the basins have taken precedence over the cattle industry. The Permian Basin designates the High Plains as one of this country's outstanding oil and gas regions. Salt, potash, and gypsum are by-product minerals the basin precipitates, but mountains, trees, crags, and waterways are missing features. Nonetheless, irrigation has permitted this land to be farmed, and vineyards near Lubbock are producing meritorious wines: Pheasant Ridge, Llano Estacado, Slaughter-Leftwich, and Cap❖Rock.

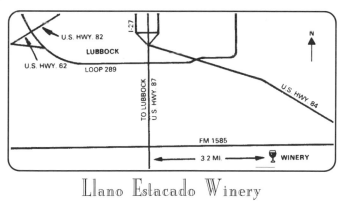

Llano Estacado Winery

Staked Plains, or in Spanish, Llano Estacado, is a giant mesa. It is called one of the most perfect plains regions in the world. It is also the name of a leading Texas winery.

A legend credits Coronado with naming the land. He came from Mexico to look for gold, and, not wanting to get lost in the featureless land, had his men drive stakes into the earth to mark the route, hence, Llano Estacado. And now Llano Estacado is an impressive, important feature on the land.

The High Plains region was accorded official appellation status in 1993. Designation as an AVA (American Viticultural Area) confirmed what the founders of Llano Estacado Winery already knew: the High Plains area surrounding Lubbock, Texas, is distinguished by the unique and favorable characteristics it lends to wine grape cultivation. With its low annual rainfall, moderate temperature, variable winds, clay loam and sandy loam soils, and high elevation of 3,000 to 4,000 feet, the High Plains region is definitely distinctive.

According to Walter Haimann, president of Llano Estacado, the wine project began with the patio grape story and Professor Bob Reed, a horticulturist at Texas Tech University.

> In the late 1950s, an experimental vineyard was uprooted to make room for a highway. Bob Reed picked up some of the discarded grapevines and took them home to make a trellis over his patio. They flourished and gave prolific yields and piqued his interest in grape growing in this area. Shortly afterwards, Dr. Clint McPherson came on campus as a chemistry professor, and his hobby was winemaking. Reed and McPherson became acquainted and fueled each other's interest in grapes, with Reed approaching it from the horticulturalist perspective and Doc (McPherson) from the winemaking perspective. They planted 100 varieties of experimental vines on ten acres not far from where the winery is today. It was a test plot for them to analyze the suitability of each variety to the climate and soil and to determine the ability of the area to produce good winemaking grapes in this environment. Incidentally, we've had grape specialists from France and America, but the grape that sparked Reed's interest has never been identified. It's called the patio grape.

McPherson decided that textbook chemistry — memorizing reactions, formulas, and such — did not capture his students' attention and enthusiasm sufficiently. In looking for a way to make the subject come alive for them, he thought about wine. As a classroom participatory demonstration, they began making wine in five-gallon jugs. Estimates of the number of compounds in wine — acids, esters, alcohols, phenols, etc. — range between 1,400 and 2,000. Wine was an effective way to teach chemistry.

In 1976, Reed, McPherson, and a group of investors founded Llano Estacado with the intention of producing the first commercial wine from the High Plains area. The first 1,300 cases were released in 1977. Those early years were difficult due to the lack of commercial wine grape vineyards. In fact, the winery building was constructed to encourage farmers to consider wine grape growing and reassure them that there was a stable market for their grapes. (Llano Estacado planted its own vineyards in 1978.)

Wine grapes are an effective product for area farmers. Today there are over 100 commercial grape growers in the High Plains, which is the largest wine grape appellation in Texas. There are currently over 3,200 acres under vine. And Llano Estacado's production has grown to 80,000 cases annually in under twenty years. Leon Adams, foremost historian on American wines, said, "There's no question the High Plains is a viticultural miracle. No one realized this area could produce world-class wines. It is an amazing story."

Nonetheless, all farming is dependent on nature, and in the High Plains the greatest fear is hail storms. Walter Haimann explained the winery's philosophy regarding hail:

> The only way to reduce hail risks is to vary vineyard selections. Hail storms are usually localized, so we look for a number of independent, dispersed grape growers and this is our solution to managing hail risk. It is our objective to do business with the most professional farmers, diversifying the locations as much as possible. The classic Bordeaux estate vineyard situation is probably not possible out here. Trying to be a winery with its own entire fruit supply would take an extraordinary risk.

Llano Estacado purchases over ninety percent of its grapes, and is the largest purchaser of Texas High Plains grapes in the state. The winery works closely with its growers, and has initiated growers' meetings for the exchange of viticultural and marketing information. "Texas wineries and grape growers can no longer depend on the chauvinistic Texas market to support sales growth. The national market must be our focus," believes Haimann. "Strong alliances between growers and producers are critical if we are going to offer wines of competitive quality, price, and prestige to go up against those from more established regions."

Greg Bruni joined Llano Estacado as winemaker in 1993, bringing three generations of California winemaking experience to the High Plains of Texas. Greg's grandfather founded California's San Martin Winery, where Greg worked since childhood. A graduate of the Enology and Viticulture Department at the famed University of California at Davis, Greg held several winemaking positions in his home state before accepting the Texas challenge.

Greg's input and advice to the growers is crucial in enhancing the viticultural procedures that will continue to improve the quality of Texas wines. He is convinced that Texas is poised to be the next major American wine region, on par with the quality appellations of California's North Coast. "I'm excited about Texas," he said. "These wines can already stand proudly next to the finest wines from California, Washington, Oregon, and abroad. And they're just going to get better and better."

At harvest, one of Greg's main objectives is to have the grapes at the winery the same day they're picked. The faster the fruit arrives and is readied for the fermentation tanks, the more control the winemaker has over the wine. In 1994, Llano Estacado began using mechanical harvesting equipment, allowing grapes to be picked in the cool of night, another quality enhancement.

No expense has been spared at Llano Estacado. The winery has the finest winemaking equipment available, including a bladder-type press. The advantage of this press is the low-pressure extraction of juice. Screw presses are efficient, perhaps more efficient than the bladder types in that they give more pressure and derive more juice per ton of grapes. But as Bruni explains:

> When you exert those tremendous pressures on a grape, you also press undesirable elements out of the grape too — like phenolics, things that make winemaking a problem from the start.

Another fine piece of equipment is Llano Estacado's Demoisy crusher. It does what a crusher should do without masticating the grapes and extracting solids with the juice. The winery also uses Mueller tanks, with a polished weld that makes it possible to keep the tanks very, very clean. Cleanliness is very important to the production of quality wine.

According to Bruni, the High Plains growers need to develop viticultural practices appropriate for their environment. The practices that have been proven in Bordeaux or Napa are not necessarily appropriate for the High Plains. Discovering those practices takes time.

> When people look at our Texas wine industry, they're impressed with what we've accomplished. But what's attracting national attention is the rate at which we've developed product excellence. We've come from the most rudimentary and fundamental grape growing and winemaking to being nationally recognized for quality wines in less than twenty years. That's an astounding rate of development.

Llano Estacado currently makes and markets twelve wines, including the popular varietals that American consumers want most: Chardonnay, Cabernet Sauvignon, Merlot, and Sauvignon Blanc. The Texas High Plains also produces excellent Chenin Blanc, Gewurtztraminer, and Johannisberg Riesling. The winery also introduced a second label of popularly priced wines in November 1993. The Staked Plains brand includes a Cabernet, Chardonnay, and Centennial Red and Centennial White, priced in the $6 to $8 range.

Llano Estacado has come a long way since its founding in 1976. In June 1986, Llano Estacado put Texas on the map when its 1984 Chardonnay captured a double gold award at the San Francisco Fair and Wine Competition, a major national competition open to wines throughout the U.S. Of 1,955 American wine entries, only eleven won double gold awards. Since 1987, Llano Estacado has received over 300 awards in national and international competitions.

There's no denying that the High Plains of Texas is an attraction. Coronado never knew what its riches really were.

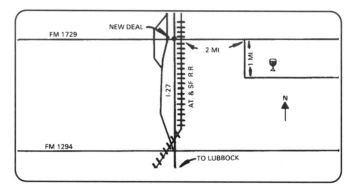

Pheasant Ridge Winery

Pheasant Ridge Winery, founded by the Robert Cox family, is an integrated vineyard/winery operation based on a commitment that premium quality *vinifera* wines can originate from the High Plains of Texas. Several years of researching the climate and soils throughout the state went into the final site selection some twenty miles north of downtown Lubbock. The first vines were planted in 1979 and the first harvest was in 1982, the year that the winery was built and named after the beautiful wild birds that roam the vineyard.

In 1986, the winery was enlarged after the Cox family partnership became a corporation and outside investors joined in ownership of the operation. Today the vineyard covers forty-eight acres and supplies most of Pheasant Ridge's 14,500 annual case production.

The Cabernet Sauvignons that Bobby Cox made for

Truchard winery, located in what is now Cat Spring, Texas, near Columbus. The brick portion of this original building extended three to four feet down into the ground to form the wine cellar (most of which has been filled in with dirt). The two-story portion is where the press was housed.

Cap❖Rock Winery

Ed and Susan Auler, Fall Creek.

Fall Creek Vineyards, Tow, Texas.

Llano Estacado Winery – Lubbock, Texas.

Greg Bruni, winemaker at Llano Estacado.

Messina Hof winemaker Paul Bonarrigo.

Messina Hof Visitors Center.

Winemaker Paul Bonarrigo in vineyards at Messina Hof.

Bottling line at the winery, Grape Creek Vineyards – Stonewall, Texas.

Richard and Bunny Becker, Becker Vineyards.

Alex Fages, vineyard manager at Ste. Genevieve.

Pheasant Ridge have been recognized for their excellence since the first release in 1983, receiving national attention as one of Texas' first two gold medals at the 1986 San Francisco Fair. Since that time, the wines have received numerous awards in national as well as state competitions. The Chardonnays have garnered medals from the Atlanta International, the Houston Club Best of Texas, and the Les Amis du Vin International wine competitions.

The quality of these wines is partly due to grapes grown in a region with the appropriate characteristics to produce fruit of intense character and ripeness. The altitude of 3,400 feet above sea level contains very dry air and rapid radiation of heat. Daytime temperatures in the growing season are in the ninety to ninety-three degree range, while the nights cool down to fifty-eight to sixty-one degrees. This cooling off each night allows the fruit to become fully ripe and intensely flavored while retaining good acidity. The vineyard soils are well-drained, fine sandy loams overlaying permeable calcareous strata. Bud break occurs in early April, and harvest begins the last week in August for Chardonnay grapes and usually lasts until the end of September with Cabernet Sauvignon. Pheasant Ridge wines have often been described as the most "French" of Texas wines with their Bordeaux-style blended Cabernets and barrel-fermented Chardonnays. The vineyard also contains Merlot, Cabernet Franc, Pinot Noir, Chenin Blanc, and Semillon grapes. The winery has one of the highest percentages of French oak storage among Texas facilities.

"We believe that nothing can replace the perfume and grace that oak lends to wine," said owner Bill Gipson. "Oak adds a nice nuance to our food-style wines, which we make with an emphasis on balance and depth."

Wine-writer Joel Flieshman reported in *Vanity Fair,* "The Pheasant Ridge Reserve Chardonnays are peers not only of California's best exemplars, but also of wines of Burgundy and Australia."

Pheasant Ridge's 1989 Proprietor's Reserve was a gold medal winner and judged Best of Show at the October 1994 "Best of Texas" annual wine event at the Houston Club in

Houston, Texas. This wine, blended and bottled in July 1994, is a Bordeaux-style blend of 54% Cabernet Sauvignon, 32% Merlot, and 14% Cabernet Franc and was aged in French oak. The same wine won "Best Red" award at the Grapefest VIP Celebrity Wine Tasting in September 1994 at Grapevine, Texas.

At this printing, management at the winery is under the direction of Bill Blackmon, and Dr. Enrique Ferro, a California wine consultant, assists on a regular basis. Bill Gipson, Jr., is in charge of marketing and serves as general manager. William E. Gipson, Sr., of Houston, is president and company chairman.

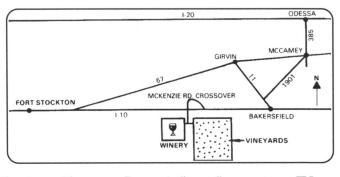

Cordier Estates, Inc. / Ste. Genevieve Wines

There have been changes at the Pecos County winery formerly called Ste. Genevieve. First, the name Ste. Genevieve now refers to a line of wines, and others will be introduced by the new owner, Domaines Cordier. It purchased the winery and vineyard operation from Bank of America in 1987. Cordier Estates, Inc., is the operating company. According to Leonard G. Garcia — president, chief executive officer, and the majority shareholder — plans are under way.

> Our partner, Domaines Cordier, is developing the vineyard in order to extend the range of our products and to complete our lines. The grapes grown in the vineyard are: Merlot, Zinfandel Gamay Noir, Pinot Noir, Cabernet Franc, Muscat, Chardonnay, Sauvignon Blanc, Chenin

Blanc, Cabernet Sauvignon, Ruby Cabernet, and Barbera. The French Colombard and part of the Chenin Blanc and Sauvignon Blanc have been overgrafted with Chardonnay, Cabernet Sauvignon, and other noble varietals.

The vineyard was developed at a cost of approximately $7 million by the University of Texas System between 1981 and 1985. The location was carefully chosen on university lands twenty-seven miles east of Fort Stockton. The success of wine grape growing at this location is attributed to several factors: generous sun exposure, a 3,000-foot elevation, well-drained alkaline topsoil, ample water from the underground aquifer, considerable difference between day and night temperatures, good climatic patterns, and a remote location which helps to prevent disease from other areas.

The vineyard was planted with 1,018 acres of varietal grapes for mostly white wines. A grafting program is in process to better balance the red and white varieties. A system of water wells, as well as their computerization, was completed before the 1988 harvest. Garcia believes water conservation is important. Much care has been put into the drip irrigation system and its automated cycle, he said, "in order to deliver the proper water supply to the plant and to save water in a very significant fashion. The vineyard is not only watered but also fertilized through the drip irrigation."

The winery was built between 1984 and 1985 by the former SGRC Corporation, along with the engineering design and expertise of Cordier France. It is regarded by national and international winery experts as a state-of-the-art system. Garcia explained their program:

> Priority is being given to putting our product back on the shelf and to refurbishing the winery. It is being upgraded now and can receive and process sixty tons of grapes per hour in order to face the necessity of having to absorb quickly the production of a two- or three-week harvest. Harvesting time is short due to the local climate. Also, we have substantial numbers of new French oak. Our next goal is to develop several lines of products to fit the different tastes and market prices. This includes a comprehensive marketing program.

Garcia believes Texas wines are very good and that within ten years Texas will be a more mature industry.

> Looking at Ste. Genevieve in the future, we see Texas wines being recognized on the same level of quality as other important American wines. We also see a new diversification in the traditional agri-business economy. When you are potentially the major player, it creates a unique opportunity to participate with the other players in the reinforcement and development of the industry and make it a successful Texas story.

For miles either side of Interstate 10 in Pecos County, level treeless country covered in scrubby brush and arid grass stretches to rising mesas that break the vast expanse of this flat land. Dry, dusty, and hot seem to describe it best. This part of West Texas is the setting for many of the Old West movies where bad guys chased good guys and the cavalry fought Indians amid a torrent of dust. It often appears little more than sage and sand enhanced only by dwarf plants, reaching endlessly in every direction.

"This is BIG COUNTRY," Jean Simmons told Gregory Peck in the movie so named, where strangers can wander lost in thousands of acres without seeing a house or a human for days. In earlier times, only the most courageous ventured to this barren semidesert which was inhabited by the Apache and Jumano tribes.

Now there's a conspicuous green patch on the landscape — caused by grapevines. Over 1,000 acres of the thriving plants are growing on the University of Texas System's land in West Texas. The objective of this plantation is wine, and the objective has been realized. Named Domaines Cordier Vineyards and Cordier Estates, Inc. Winery, the cooperative effort is producing good Cabernet Sauvignon, Chardonnay, Merlot, Gamay Beaujolais, White Zinfandel, Chenin Blanc, Sauvignon Blanc, Texas White, Texas Red, and other wines first made available to the public in the autumn of 1985 under the Ste. Genevieve label. Many people express disbelief when they learn of the university's wine project and wonder how it came to be.

In the mid-nineteenth century, the debt incurred by

Texas' War for Independence and the early years of the Republic needed to be repaid. To raise the money, Texas sold portions of land that would become parts of New Mexico, Oklahoma, Kansas, Colorado, and Wyoming, but strangely, it did not sell the rugged West. Texas retained it and eventually designated fifty leagues of the public domain as a permanent provision of support for schools and colleges.

In 1876, the Texas Constitution provided for a "university of the first class" and one million acres were set aside in West Texas for that purpose. The second million acres were added to it in 1883, and although it must have appeared worthless to those hungry for revenue from productive land to fund education, their most extravagant hopes were fulfilled when oil was discovered there in 1923. The consequent production from the aggregate oil wells has helped provide an endowment that is the second largest of any university in the United States. And according to Billy Carr, retired manager of University Lands-Surface Interests, the vines on that land are also helping to repay a debt.

> Maybe the concept comes out of the two billion plus dollars we have taken out of this land in royalty and oil. The idea was to put some money back — not directly, but indirectly — to preserve and protect it. Our program started here because we felt we ought to have full utilization of our land. We began at first with range conservation, trying to utilize our range land better. And we were very successful with the soil conservation. The USDA Soil Conservation Service helped, and we probably doubled the production of livestock. So the next step was to consider what we might do better for other crops, something that would provide a higher income. Back ten years ago we planted many crops — olives, kiwi vines, walnuts, grapes, anything we could think of that would work on a drip irrigation system and use less water. But grapes from the time we planted them in Van Horn, Texas, and moved on here to Bakersfield have never looked bad. They were on and on good, and we finally made wine . . . the wine has turned out excellently.

If making wine from grapes grown in an area that is known as the most arid section of Texas seems hard to believe, the project is possible because of drip irrigation. Primitive methods of irrigating have been used since prehistoric times, but trickle or drip irrigation is a more recent tool of modern technology. The source came from renewable underground water supplies. Its existence was recognized by the number of productive farms in Pecos County with working wells. In 1974, Billy Carr and the land management office and the UT Board of Regents decided to find better ways to utilize the land and the water. At that time, drip irrigation was beginning to be recognized as a good irrigation method where water supplies were limited. And grapes, of all perennial crops that might grow well in West Texas, seemed to have the most potential for a high economic return. So an experimental vineyard was planted near Van Horn in Culberson County in March 1975 to determine if commercially acceptable quality grapes could be grown, which varieties were the best to grow, and what type of irrigation system was best. The conclusion was Ste. Genevieve Wines. Carr traced the development:

> We proved we could grow the grapes and make the wine, so the next step was to decide what we were going to do with it, either go commercial or drop it. I presented the proposal to go commercial to the board of regents, and after that we hired the firm of Booz, Allen and Hamilton to make a survey on the economics of it. The survey came back positive with a lot of caution added to it. So the board felt it was time to go ahead with the plan and I was ready, too. I felt real comfortable that we could do this and make it go. Well, probably the board, bless their hearts, stuck their necks out with me, 'cause we planted 640 acres before we had a contract. Luckily it worked out real well.

The commercial vineyard at Bakersfield was initially named Escondido Vineyards (which means hidden) after the Escondido Ranch upon which the vineyards were planted and the Escondido Springs, an early stagecoach stop in the area. In 1981, eighty acres each of Chenin Blanc and French Colombard were planted, followed by the planting of an additional 160 acres in 1982, 230 acres in 1983, and 360 acres in 1984 – for a total of nine different grape varieties.

In 1982 and 1983, negotiations with in-state, national, and international companies were conducted in order to find a commercial operator of the vineyards and an owner and operator of a commercial winery sufficiently large to process all of the grapes from the commercial vineyards. In late June 1983, a lease agreement was signed between UT and a partnership called Gill-Richter-Cordier, Inc., put together by Richardson (Dick) Gill. The initial partners were Gill, the Richter Company of Montpellier, France, and Domaines Cordier of Bordeaux, France. In 1984, the A. R. Sanchez family of Laredo, Texas, joined the Texas/French partnership which then became SGRC, Ltd. SGRC, Ltd. chose to operate under the name Ste. Genevieve Vineyards. The first Ste. Genevieve wines were marketed in August 1985.

Among other factors, the declining Texas economy put a financial strain on SGRC, Ltd. to the point that UT took over the operation of Ste. Genevieve in October 1986. The grapes and the wine did not know that the Texas economy was hurting. They kept on growing and producing fine wines.

In 1987 one of the original partners, Domaines Cordier, formed a partnership with a French-born Texan named John Collet of San Antonio. Their new company was Cordier Estates, Inc. It and Domaines Cordier negotiated a new contract with UT for the lease of the vineyards and the ownership of the winery. In October 1987, Cordier Estates, Inc., took over the ownership and operation of the winery, which is called Cordier Estates Winery. Domaines Cordier leases and operates the vineyards. The wine is still sold under the Ste. Genevieve Vineyards label, and a percentage of every bottle of wine sold will go to the state of Texas' Permanent University Fund to support higher education in Texas.

In 1993 Don Brady became the winemaker. He is the most awarded winemaker in Texas. Jean Louis Haberer, who has been with the winery since the beginning, directs the vineyard operations and is a technical adviser at the winery. He conducts harvests in Austria, France, and New Zealand as well.

Wine, of course, begins with the vine and the soil. They are the constants. Climate determines the character possibilities, and sometimes weather can exclude the winemaker from that determination. Dr. Charles McKinney, director of research for the University Lands-Surface Interests Office, believes the important factors occur in West Texas.

> Grapes respond to climatic conditions, and a combination of warm days and cool nights helps to develop and intensify the distinctive taste characteristics of the variety, called the varietal character. The Pecos County vineyards enjoy an ideal climate at their nearly 2,700-foot elevation. Grapes are harvested over about a four-week period, usually mid-July to mid-August. Vines require about twenty-six inches of moisture per year. Natural rainfall in the area is about ten to twelve inches per year, with some years as low as three inches. But the area is blessed with an underground water supply—the Trinity Water Table— that provides the additional water to irrigate vineyards.

McKinney said vineyard cultivation begins with the vines. They respond well to the soil, which is calcareous or limestone based, a silty clay loam. The soil is powdery when dry and the sort that is used to make adobe bricks. It is slick when wet, but there is good percolation or water penetration. The calcareous soils do require the addition of iron and zinc in order to get full plant development.

E. E. (Gene) Drennan, vineyard manager for the University Lands-Surface Interests Office, planted and developed the commercial vineyards for UT. He cared for the vines until they were three years old or until they started producing grapes. The fruit is taken off the plant the first and second year to enhance the vines. When vines are two years old, they are shaped and will retain that shape for life. The third year, often called the third leaf, is the first crop for Texas vines. French law requires that the first crop for *appellation contrôlée* wine must come from four-year-old vines. The first growth wines of Bordeaux, *Grand Crus Classé*, don't use vines less than eight years old. The older the vine, the finer (but less in amount) is the wine. Few wineries can afford to wait that long before they make wine.

"Out here we get ninety percent optimal yield in the sixth year," McKinney said, "and optimal yield most years from the seventh on. We also have eight feet between plants and twelve feet between rows for 454 plants per acre."

Such luxury with the land only happens with an abundance of it available. In Burgundy, France, for example, the famous Côte de Nuits region contains approximately 3,700 acres of vine. That amount of total acreage is divided among 419 vineyards, which means the average size of a Côte de Nuits vineyard is about 8.9 acres. Vines are planted forty inches apart, and there are about six feet between rows. The largest vineyard in the area is Clos de Vougeot with 125 acres, and the smallest one is Les Meix Bas with 1.2 acres. The tremendous amounts of space between plants and rows and the amount of land allocated to roads in West Texas is unique. It permits the use of mechanical harvesters and other equipment that together with the latest technology and state-of-the-art winery make Ste. Genevieve very impressive indeed.

Another big difference between the two wine regions of West Texas and Burgundy is geographic latitude; Pecos County is 30°N and Burgundy's Côte de Nuits is 48°N. Pecos runs on a latitudinal line that crosses Algeria, Arabia, and Iran, while the Côte de Nuits line crosses Mongolia and Winnipeg. Vines require fifty degrees Fahrenheit (ten degrees Centigrade) for growth, so whether they grow in a warmer or colder region, McKinney says the important thing is for the temperature to be sufficiently warm during the growing season.

> In the spring, as soon as the average daily temperature reaches about fifty-five degrees Fahrenheit, the dormant vine begins to grow and put out shoots. Bud-break at Ste. Genevieve Vineyards occurs in mid-March. Flower clusters emerge with the new shoots, and about forty-five days later, the flowers bloom. Soon after, the flowers are replaced by small, hard, green, tart berries. The berries grow rapidly for a time, until the beginning of ripening,

and then continue more gradually afterwards. When cell division in the berries has ceased, a second period of growth — cell enlargement — begins. From this stage until the fruit is ripe, the grapes become larger and sweeter.

Grapes are different sizes and shapes and they vary in weight. Chenin Blanc clusters weigh about ¾ pound a cluster while Chardonnay clusters weigh about ⁴⁄₁₀ pound. Of course, in nature there are no absolutes. The expected yields vary considerably from vineyard site to vineyard site. They depend on cultural practices and the age of the vine. The weight of the cluster depends on the overall number of pounds on the plant, McKinney said, adding:

> All these things are highly variable. . . . We expect the Chenin Blanc to produce about ten tons per acre. Barbera seven tons, French Colombard nine tons, Chardonnay four to five tons. But a lot of the measurement should be per plant rather than per acre because there are different numbers of plants per acre in different vineyards. We have 454 plants per acre. Also, production depends on the richness of the soil and the weight of clusters in relation to the vigor of the plant. A grape's preference for a particular climate is determined by the rapidity with which it matures and the chemistry balance. In cold areas that have a short growing season they must have grapes that can grow and mature in a hurry and in warmer climates it's a more leisurely process. Henri Bernabé, the partner who owns the international vine nursery in France, says our weather is perfect and that the difference in day and night temperatures is especially desirable.

Even though many of those involved in the West Texas wine project are Frenchmen, they are not trying to produce a French wine. It will be a Texas-style wine with characteristics of the region, a premium wine. Carr says he has never felt as if they were in competition with the French.

> What we probably have competition with is that we know we have to match California wines to even hit a market here, because that's the market. Leon Adams [authority

on American wines and author] has said our wines are comparable to the coastal wines below Napa or in some cases some of ours are hitting close to Napa's. Most of the wine experts have pretty well keyed us in to being comparable to those wines.

In late 1991, processing and blending wines changed at Ste. Genevieve and there was also a new label and packaging. Since then, sales have grown from 42,000 cases in Texas in 1991 to more than 200,000 cases in 1994, making Ste. Genevieve the largest selling Texas wine. Ste. Genevieve is the number-one selling Chardonnay and the Cabernet Sauvignon is the number-two selling Cabernet in the San Antonio and Austin markets.

Texas wines are unique. They will reflect the character of the land and the essence of the grape grown on that land and in that climate. The expression "you are what you eat" applies to grapes, too. Perhaps Charles McKinney said it best: "A good winemaker saves what was in the vineyard and a poor one doesn't."

Ste. Genevieve wines have won numerous state, national, and international awards and continue to do so.

STE. GENEVIEVE WINE AWARDS
1994 Awards

Sauvignon Blanc Non-Vintage	Number One, 1.5 Liter Division	1994 *Dallas Morning News* National Wine Competition
White Zinfandel Non-Vintage	Number One, 1.5 Liter Division	1994 *Dallas Morning News* National Wine Competition
Chenin Blanc Non-Vintage	Silver Medal	1994 Texas Wine Classic
Proprietor's Reserve 1992 Chardonnay	Silver Medal	1994 Texas Wine Classic
Sauvignon Blanc Non-Vintage	Silver Medal	1994 Texas Wine Classic
Chardonnay Non-Vintage	Bronze Medal	1994 Texas Wine Classic
Proprietor's Reserve 1991 Cabernet Sauvignon	Bronze Medal	1994 Texas Wine Classic

Classic White	Bronze Medal	1994 Texas Wine Classic
Proprietor's Reserve 1992 Chardonnay	Silver Medal	International Eastern Wine Competition (Watkins Glen, NY)
White Zinfandel Non-Vintage	Silver Medal	International Eastern Wine Competition (Watkins Glen, NY)
Proprietor's Reserve 1991 Cabernet Sauvignon	Bronze Medal	International Eastern Wine Competition (Watkins Glen, NY)
Chenin Blanc Non-Vintage	Bronze Medal	International Eastern Wine Competition (Watkins Glen, NY)

1995 Awards

Cabernet Sauvignon Non-Vintage	Gold Medal	San Diego National Wine Competition
White Zinfandel Non-Vintage	Gold Medal	New World International Wine Competition
Merlot Non-Vintage	Silver Medal	New World International Wine Competition
Texas White Non-Vintage	Silver Medal	New World International Wine Competition
Cabernet Sauvignon Non-Vintage	Bronze Medal	New World International Wine Competition

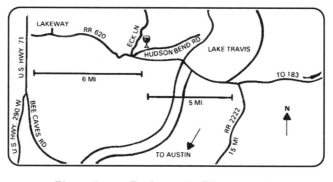

Slaughter-Leftwich Vineyards

George Webb Slaughter was the private courier and scout to Sam Houston. He delivered Houston's urgent message to Travis at the Alamo, telling him to evacuate or die. Returning a reply message from Travis to Houston, the courier was also the last of those brave men to leave the Alamo alive.

"I'm glad he didn't stay because I sure wouldn't be here if he had," smiled Scott Slaughter, descendant and managing director of Slaughter-Leftwich Vineyards.

The vineyards are in Lubbock and the winery is in Austin. It's a unique combination, but it works effectively for Slaughter and his family. Slaughter said his mother, June Leftwich Slaughter (now Mrs. Ben Head), was the guiding force behind the vineyard adventure: "She encouraged me, financed it, and is involved in all the day-to-day operations."

The project began when Scott graduated from Texas Tech. His family had been in the ranching and farming business for generations, and he decided he wanted an agricultural connection.

> I was looking for intensive rather than extensive agricultural pursuits. I'd research the land and then the family would go look at the property. One trip was to the Hill Country to consider pecan trees. Then our banker told us he had a friend who was convinced about a wine grape industry in Texas. So we investigated in our area around Lubbock and that's how we met the professors at Llano Estacado: Clint McPherson, Robert Reed, and Roy Mitchell.

The three Tech professors had collaborated on the viticulture and vinification that evolved into Llano Estacado Winery. The Slaughters became general partners and wanted to buy land close to the winery and in a wet area for future possibilities. June Leftwich Slaughter purchased eighty acres one-fourth of a mile from Llano Estacado, and son Scott went to work in the vineyards.

> That summer of 1978 I learned to train the vines at Llano Estacado with horticulturalist Bob Reed. I was more than ready for September. My family took a trip to Napa to see the established vineyards and wineries because we had decided to go into the commercial wine grape business. Then we ordered plants in the winter and the following spring, 1979, we planted our vineyards.

Forty-five acres were planted to vines with twelve acres of hybrids, eight acres of Chardonnay, ten acres of Chenin Blanc, eight acres of Ruby Cabernet, and seven of Petit Sirah. It was a tremendous undertaking for the graduate-turned-vineyardist. The acreage included 25,000 plants.

> It takes time to tie up the vines. A lot of time. That first year we planted the vines and farmed cotton between the vines, which were planted on an eight-by-twelve grid. Ninety-eight percent of the vines survived. The following year we drove the stakes and trained the vines up on the wires. Shortly afterwards, on June 30, 1980, when they were all trained, a hail storm mowed them to the ground. It was the middle of summer, so I tied them up again. That winter we had terrible weather and they froze to the ground. Then the following spring, 1981, we trained them up again. That was three times I had to tie up about 25,000 vines. I felt like I personally had trained the labor force in Lubbock to do that job.

There was a good Chardonnay harvest in 1982, so the decision was made that same year to T-bud the twelve acres of hybrids to Chardonnay and Cabernet Sauvignon. Incidentally, it was the Slaughter-Leftwich Chardonnay that Kim McPherson (now at Texas Vineyards) used for the 1984 Llano Estacado that won the double gold medal at the San Francisco Fair. Slaughter said that for the four years that Llano Estacado used their grapes, they won more medals than any other vineyard in the state.

> I was vice-president and a director of Llano Estacado during their infancy and expansion, and I gained a lot of practical information. I took courses at U.C. Davis too, but I also learned through the process of doing. For example, the Petit Sirah was too weak to even T-bud, so I pulled up all of it. It took us forever to get out of that forty-five acres of initial vines because I kept having to redo so much. Now I know better, but at the time I was pioneering. We have fifty acres now, with five acres of Chardonnay planted in the spring of 1988.

Slaughter-Leftwich Vineyards incorporated in 1985 and the family decided to build its own winery. Scott spent six months looking for a winery site and then decided to build in the Hill Country in the spring of 1986. Two reasons were that Austin is the number-one tourist attraction city and the number-one per capita fine wine consumption city in the state. In 1986 and 1987, Slaughter-Leftwich used the facilities at Llano Estacado and Cypress Valley to make its wine. "We wanted to have wine available for our tours and tasting when we opened our new facility on Lake Travis in October 1988," Slaughter explained.

The winery, situated on eleven acres which overlooks Lake Travis, has a special view. The finest equipment has been purchased for the winery, and Scott believes they can produce the highest quality wine from their Lubbock fruit.

> We grow the best wine grapes produced in Texas. We've already won several medals: "Best of Show" at the Houston Club Competition for the 1986 Slaughter-Leftwich Chardonnay; a silver at the Houston Club for our 1986 Sauvignon Blanc; and a bronze medal in the Lone Star Competition for our 1986 Austin Blush. The 1993 Sauvignon Blanc won a gold medal in the 10th Annual *Dallas Morning News* Wine Competition. And numerous medals continue to be awarded to our wines.

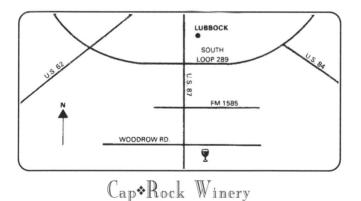

Cap❖Rock Winery

Cap❖Rock Winery, a Texas High Plains wine operation southeast of Lubbock, is named for an area geological formation. Below the top soil and clay of this high plateau region lies an impervious stratum of resistant rock called a caprock.

Above the flatness of this vast land rises Cap✦Rock Winery, an architecturally stunning, Southwestern-mission-style winery built in 1988. Having the best modern equipment encourages excellent quality control and innovation. Cap✦Rock has options like pressing whole berry clusters, which keeps freshness in the richer wines, and a juice chiller, which preserves the wine's fruity character.

The Texas High Plains has an international reputation for growing superb *vinifera* grapes. At 3,400 feet elevation, the climate is semi-arid and mild with cool nights and warm days — ideal conditions for growing sound grapes. Most of the eighteen to nineteen inches of annual rainfall occurs between May and June, a benefit since harvest begins in early August and ends in September.

Grapes (Chardonnay, Sauvignon Blanc, Chenin Blanc, Pinot Blanc, Cabernet Sauvignon, Merlot, Pinot Noir, and Riesling) for Cap✦Rock wines come from its own 119-acre vineyard and selected area growers, both under the careful management of viticulturist Mark Penna. With the purchase of a mechanical picker in 1994, Penna now harvests long before sunrise, preserving the quality of the fruit by gathering it in the cool early morning hours.

Initially called Teysha Winery, Cap✦Rock is owned by Plains Capital Corporation of Lubbock. It took over the operation in 1989 and changed the name in 1992. The first major decision was to hire winemaker Kim McPherson, a member of a pioneering Texas wine family. His father, Dr. Clinton McPherson, and Bob Reed founded Llano Estacado Winery in 1975, where Kim also made wine and created the 1984 Llano Estacado from the Slaughter-Leftwich Vineyard that won a double gold medal at the San Francisco Fair in 1986 and brought international attention to Texas wines. Through Kim's career at several wineries, his wines have won more than 300 medals in competitions around the U.S.

The next consideration was a distinctive label. Elizabeth Pressler of St. Helena, California, took the colors and contours of the caprock and the play of light from Texas sunsets to design a striking, award-winning label.

Jay Alvis and his marketing company, Southwestern Marketing, was hired to add insight, pricing, promotion, and marketing techniques to help position Cap✦Rock among the many wines in the "fighting varietals" category.

The Cap✦Rock product line consists of twelve wines divided into four tiers:

Tier I — Sparkling, Brut, Methode Champenoise (first release won a gold at Orange County Fair in California); Reserve Cabernet Sauvignon; Reserve Chardonnay (Reserves are made only in exceptional years)

Tier II — Cabernet Sauvignon; Chardonnay; Cabernet Royale, Proprietary wine, Cabernet Sauvignon

Tier III — Sauvignon Blanc; Chenin Blanc; Tapestry, Proprietary wine, Sauvignon Blanc/Semillon

Tier IV — Red Table; White Table; Blush Table

In 1994 John Bratcher joined the team at Cap✦Rock to direct sales and marketing. John worked with Kim at Llano Estacado for several years and the two were glad to be reunited.

"We enjoy doing work that returns something to our hometown and to Texas," Bratcher explained. "The old 'Texas Spirit' is alive and well, but Texas wines are good enough now to stand on their own. The fact that our grapes are grown in the Lubbock area, primarily by farmers, has made wine drinking very acceptable even though Lubbock is very much in the 'Bible belt.' I know a lot of people who will order a glass of Cap✦Rock in a restaurant who would never order a beer or mixed drink. When my dad introduced me to his preacher in Plainview, Texas, and told him I worked for a Lubbock winery, I knew we were going to make it."

The planning and development of Cap✦Rock continues to assure a bright and promising future. The 1995 production is extimated at over 30,000 cases with a capacity of 55,000 cases. The building has the space to increase production to approximately 85,000 cases. The winery is projected to grow to over 50,000 cases before 2000 A.D. Because of the superior equipment at Cap✦Rock, the winery does custom crushing for other wineries that contract grapes in the High Plains area.

AWARDS: "Best Buy" Cabernet Sauvignon for 1994,

Wine & Spirits (one of only twelve such recommendations);
Gold Medal, 1993 Cabernet Royale, International Eastern
Wine Competition, Watkins Glen, NY and named as the
"Texas State Champion Wine"; Gold Medal and "Best of
Show" for the NV Sparkling, Houston Club's "Best of
Texas"; Gold Medal at the National Orange Show; Gold
Medal and "Star of Texas Grand Award—Best Red Wine" at
the Lone Star State Wine Competition, 1991 Cabernet
Sauvignon; Gold Medal, "Best Abstract Wine Label Presen-
tation," New World International Wine Competition; An-
thony Dias Blue's "Summer White Sale" in *Bon Appetit* (July
1994), Sauvignon Blanc.

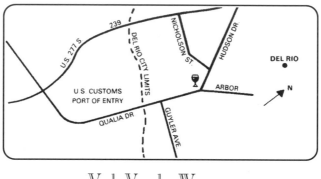

Val Verde Winery

Passports were not readily available in Italy during the
1870s. Nonetheless, the king's agent did issue scrolls, and
Francis (Frank) Qualia received one to emigrate. A native of
northern Italy, he joined a group led by a Lombardic count
who had been given a grant by the king to establish a colony
in Mexico.

About all the Italians brought with them was a knowledge of working the land and willingness to do it. But
Mexico did not meet their expectations, and the ill-fated
colony did not survive into the 1880s.

Several disappointed colonists, including Qualia, went
to Texas. They had heard the San Antonio climate was
agreeable and the land abundant and rich. When they arrived, however, they found that the best land had been

taken. Tired but undaunted, they sent scouts to find land suitable for orchards, vineyards, and other preferred crops. In the meantime, Qualia and the other men worked on a section of the New York, Texas and Mexican Railway that ran between Rosenberg and Victoria. Reports came down the line, as well as from the scouts, about the border city on the Rio Grande. Qualia decided to take a look at Del Rio.

Hans Mickle reported in the *San Antonio Daily Express*, January 24, 1883:

> This [Del Rio] undoubtedly is one of the future greats of Western Texas. It is 170 miles from San Antonio and is the point where the railroad reaches the Rio Grande. . . . Sixteen years ago (1867), a man named Taylor moved several Mexican families here along with his Mexican wife and opened the San Felipe Farms, which were irrigated by water taken from nearby San Felipe Springs. . . . 2,800 acres are under cultivation and 2,000 more could easily be added.

Taylor's widow, who was also the widow of a Dr. Rivera, Dona Paula Losoya de Rivera, was managing the fertile lands of her hacienda when Qualia arrived in 1882. He admired the well-tended vineyards and was given cuttings to begin his own grape agriculture. The stock was the Lenoir, and it is still cultivated in the Qualia vineyards by Frank Qualia's grandson, Tommy Qualia, the present owner-producer of Val Verde Winery.

"My grandfather thought Del Rio was a farmer's place," Tommy Qualia said, "a good place to settle and grow crops, especially vines."

Frank Qualia purchased ten acres from some Spanish settlers, and the land included a vineyard. He was fascinated with the idea of creating his own table wines and founded his winery in 1883.

The initial venture was simply to provide wines for his family, but as guests were invited to his table, the reputation of his wine spread. Friends and neighbors wanted to buy his wine, so Qualia increased his production and went commercial. All winemakers are bonded and regulated by the state and federal governments. Qualia's wine barrels posted liquor stamps he had purchased from the federal government.

"My grandfather died in 1926," Tommy Qualia said. "Then my father, Louis, took over the vineyards. He introduced the Herbemont grape into our winery in the 1930s."

Prohibition didn't kill Frank Qualia, but it probably broke his heart. Of the thirty to forty wineries and vineyards in Texas in 1920, all disappeared during the dry decade.

"As far as I know, my father and grandfather were the only winemakers who continued to give care to their vineyards during Prohibition," Qualia said. "After Repeal, my father began operating the winery in 1933. Our legal number is Permit No. 17. All the earlier numbers were discontinued because of Prohibition, or we'd be number one."

Louis Qualia turned over Val Verde Winery and the operation to his son Tommy several years before his death in 1981. The third-generation Qualia respects the efforts and expertise that preceded him. He continues to experiment with plant adaptability and disease-resisting factors, but at the same time, he reveres his heritage and perpetuates it.

"The winery building is the original adobe brick," Qualia said. "It's been enlarged, but it's the same structure my grandfather and father used."

Other historical items reflect the Qualia family pride in their heritage, such as the old wine press that Frank Qualia bought. It was made in Italy during the 1870s. Until ten years ago, the press initiated every harvest. There are, however, some 1870 vintages that still are used—Spanish sherry barrels that hold Val Verde wine. Of course, it takes a lot of new barrels, too.

"We're expanding our vineyards and studying ways to improve our grapes," Qualia said. "Authorities say we can't grow grapes permanently in Texas, but our hybrids are doing beautifully and I sure aim to prove them wrong."

After 100 years of successful winemaking, it appears Tommy Qualia has a historical precedent that just may prove the authorities were mistaken.

6

Guide to
Texas Wines

Satisfy your hearts with food and wine,
for therein is courage and strength.
– Homer, *The Iliad*

The Texas wine industry has taken a lot of people by surprise. Some are still learning about it. After they do, mouths drop open, eyes get wider, and brows rise with comments like "Cabernet from cow country?" or "Bubba's Yellow Rose of Texas?" or "Chicken fried steak and Château de l'Alamo?"

Well, many of those skeptics have been drinking Texas wine for several years now and their comments have changed. The wine has improved. And not only that, it just keeps getting better and better. Texans have done their homework, and their winemaking skills are impressive.

The Lone Star state's wine industry is not new, however. It's actually older than California's by as much as 100 years. It began in 1659 with the establishment of a mission at El Paso; experienced ups and downs for a couple of centuries; received international recognition when T. V. Munson, a nineteenth-century horticulturist from Denison, helped restore devastated vineyards in France; and then died during Prohibition. The big problem with Texas wine during this time was the grape. Native Texas grapes didn't produce a product nearly as fine as the wine grapes from Europe. Unfortunately, the European varieties died in Texas soil.

A major year in the rejuvenation of the Texas wine industry was 1975. That was the year that test plots of vines proved European wine grapes could thrive in Texas. Technology, especially drip irrigation, improved the chances for survival, but in the main, vines had previously been planted in the wrong places. Now wine comes from an estimated 2,500 acres of mature vines. That's not a lot of wine. In California's Napa Valley, for example, 30,000 acres produce 100,000 tons of grapes, and Champagne, France, has 84,000 acres with 64,000 producing. Although some Texas wine is shipped out of state, the precious few bottles are sold at home almost as soon as they come off the bottling line. Consequently, Texans are the privileged imbibers, and they're enjoying "the next big thing from Texas" at celebrations, banquets, parties, and dinners around the state. Entertaining has an added dimension.

ENTERTAINING WITH TEXAS WINES

Texas hospitality, of course, is legendary, and now with so many delicious Texas wines on the market, friendly gatherings just keep getting better. Whether you're entertaining a herd or a handful or merely serving an intimate twosome, there's a Texas wine to suit your dinner, lunch, picnic — or as an aperitif.

A lovely way to begin any evening is with champagne. Sparkling wine has the distinction of being delicious alone or with any course of a meal. Texas offers sparkling wine from several areas, and they're worthy of starting the evening well.

Bubbly wines are marvelous with soft-ripened cheeses such as Coulommiers and Brie or their comparable but richer friends which the French call *double crèmes* or *triple crèmes*. Defined by law, these must contain sixty percent and seventy-two percent more fat respectively. The French like to have cheese just before dessert, and many Texans do likewise. A more common practice, however, is to serve a tray of assorted cheeses with an aperitif. If the setting is a party, the selection should include mild and firm cheeses that are easy to slice and eat while standing. For example, Port Salut,

Havarti, Muenster, Monterey Jack, Jarlsberg, Emmenthaler, Provolone, Cheddar, Colby, and Edam are all convenient appetizer cheeses and may be served with bread or crackers. Properly wrapped and stored, they should keep for a couple of weeks. With these cheeses serve both fruity white wines and medium bodied red wines such as Riesling, Chenin Blanc, Chardonnay, Gamay, and proprietary red wines, Pinot Noir, and Merlot.

For cheeses served before dessert or as dessert, offer the soft-ripened ones and members of the blue family. With Roquefort, Pipo Crem, Gorgonzola, Stilton, and other blues there are several suitable wines. The British like Stilton and port; the French like sauternes and Roquefort; Americans prefer a sturdy Medoc (Cabernet Sauvignon) or Côte de Nuits (Pinot Noir) with blue cheeses, while I frequently choose a champagne. All this points out the fact that food and wine marriages are subjective, and personal preference ought always to be the major criterion. Nonetheless, recommended for the soft-ripened and blue cheeses are Cabernet Sauvignon, Zinfandel, Merlot, and Pinot Noir.

Entertaining is simplified when guests serve themselves and the food choices are ample but limited. A salad of mixed greens and herbs (with a cream, oil, or cheese dressing, not vinegar), fresh bread, a main course with rice, egg noodles, beans or potatoes can fill a plate and satisfy your hungriest visitor, especially when the offering is Texas Wine Beef (see recipe) served with a Cabernet Sauvignon, Carnelian, Merlot, or other red wine.

Barbecued ham is a great party item. Hams are easily prepared, serve small or large groups, and can be enjoyed right off the pit. Frequently, though, hams come in sizes which can be a leftover problem. Serve the leftovers in Sweet and Sour Holiday Ham (see recipe) on a bed of fluffy rice. With a cup of potato and parsley soup (see recipe) and hot rolls, the meal is complete. Try the ham with Chenin Blanc, Gewurztraminer, or Riesling.

If the preference is for chicken, try oven-grilled broilers. They are excellent with fresh mushrooms filled with buttery, crisp garden green peas, and a spicy dressing on the plate. Serve Chardonnay and light-bodied reds with the broilers.

Almost everyone likes a touch of something sweet at the end of a meal. A platter filled with a variety of confections is a gracious offering because it lets guests select as many or as few sweets as they want. Another tempting sweet is Texas Buttermilk Pie (see recipe). Served with a Texas sparkling wine, it always makes a good finale. For a perfect finish, try a glass of port. There are several of these rich, smooth drinks.

Here's an additional tip on serving wines to your guests: The use of multiple wines and multiple glasses appears to be increasingly infrequent. If two wines are served, and encouragement is given for the practice, begin with a chilled, fifty-degree white wine and then serve the red wine at sixty degrees. Even in the coolest Texas houses, wines will exceed their best drinking temperatures shortly after being poured. Keep the wines (even reds) in a bucket filled with half water and half ice for fifteen minutes before serving. If one wine will accompany the entire meal, it should complement the main course. The one glass suitable for all wines is approved by the International Standards Organization (ISO) and appropriately called the ISO glass. It is a stemmed, closed-tulip-shaped glass approximately six and one-fourth inches in height and holds about eight ounces. Fill the glass one-third to one-half full. This amount permits one to swirl the wine in order to sniff the bouquet without spilling.

FOOD AND WINE: CREATING THE PERFECT MATCH

Texas has numerous wineries now that produce a variety of vintages. Even though Texans have a preference for the chilled whites, there's a growing admiration for Texas reds. White or red, good wine enhances good food; however, a few guidelines make the process of matching food and wine easier and more enjoyable.

The adage "Use red wines with red meat and white with white" is just a little too simple. While it is generally true that fish, chicken, and other such meats go nicely with white wine, the way a dish is prepared is more significant. For example, chicken sautéed in butter requires a light, fresh, white wine. On the other hand, chicken prepared with garlic and heavy spices needs a red or white wine with a definite and prevailing flavor. With beef, game, or pasta with meat sauce, reds are recommended because red wines are dry (with exceptions), and such dishes require dry, not sweet, wine.

Experimentation and tradition have established some general rules over the years that make sense. One guide matches food and wine from the same region. The association works fine in France, where a region or district has a predominant wine, but not in Texas, where one vineyard may produce five or ten varieties. Also, the habit of pairing local wines and foods was convenient when one had to wait on the carriage or the caravan to make alternate selections. But the advent of modern transportation has changed the Old World approach to gustatory delights.

Some things don't change, however, and one basic rule concerning food and wine is that flavors should complement, not overpower, each other. The progression of wines usually proceeds from light, fresh whites to dry and full-bodied whites; then lighter reds followed by sturdier ones; strongest wines with strongest flavors, especially cheeses; and sweet wines for dessert.

Before getting into more detailed food and wine combinations, let me preface by saying that my suggestions are just that — suggestions. There shouldn't be hard and fast rules, in my opinion, about pairing food and wine except the personal preference of the individual. If you like, there are certain classic combinations that you can taste to educate your palate: champagne and caviar, Chablis and oysters, sauternes and foie gras, port and Stilton, Bordeaux and lamb, Chardonnay and lobster, white burgundy and quenelles, and Chianti and pasta. Basically, though, drink whatever wine tastes good to you with the food you like to have accompany it. Apart from that note, chemistry shows some interesting reasons why certain wines and foods go well together.

For example, foods that are high in protein have a soothing, softening effect on tannin. Fat also subdues tannin. That is why assertive young Bordeaux or Rhone red wines can stand up to strong cheeses and hearty meat dishes. That is not to say that the mellowing which age brings to wine in any way detracts from pairing older red wines with beef, game, and cheese. Far from it. Older Grande Cru Classe Bordeaux or American Cabernet Sauvignon wines complement grilled or roasted beef, venison, lamb, duck, and so forth very well. These superlative wines are extremely suitable for simply prepared, straightforward meats which can tend to accentuate the roughness of younger wines. Another thing about young wines — tannins in high concentration can mask the fruit and other flavors as well as acidity. Although younger wines can be difficult to pair due to strong tannins, they are less expensive and more plentiful, so it's especially nice to know how to use them. Also, modern technology and production methods are making red wines more approachable when released.

Again, sauces and garnishes dictate wine selections more than the meat. Fine quality pieces of beef or lamb, for example, seldom need excessive garniture. They tend to stand on their own merit. It is more the nature of chicken, seafood, bland meat, and cheese dishes to be mixed with a number of ingredients that confuse the wine issue. In such instances either try to match the dominant flavor or let the wine take a back seat to the piquant and full-flavored food. It's better than having the wine and food fight for dominance.

Two things that decrease the perception of sweetness in wine are cold and acid. High acidity makes wine seem less sweet, and colder temperatures do the same thing. Sweetness also calms hotness. That's why a chilled Riesling is often nice with Mexican food. Champagne is another of my wine preferences with Mexican food. There is a contrast and cleansing of palate that I find refreshing with the match.

A word of caution: One should be careful when pairing wines with certain foods. These include salads with acidulous dressing (or any other vinegar-based relish or condiment), anchovies, fresh tomatoes, fresh citrus fruits, kippers, and some would add asparagus and artichokes.

Otherwise, fill the glass one-third to one-half full, and enjoy.

IT'S A MATTER OF TASTE

Getting to know your wines begins with a wine vocabulary. The terms really are essential for describing the wines you taste. I would begin, however, by keeping it simple. Is it really necessary to use ten or more adjectives to describe a wine? Remember, you smell at least eighty-five percent of what you taste. It's logical when you think about it. The tongue distinguishes only four tastes: sweet, acid, salty, and bitter. But the average nose can smell 4,000 odors. The mouth feels for balance and structure, the texture of the wine. Wines differ in body; that is, in substance. Full-bodied wines are mouth filling and give an impression of being viscous or weighty rather than thin and watery. Light and medium-bodied wines are measured by degrees in the opposite direction from full-bodied. For example, try a Fall Creek Emerald Riesling and compare this light, fresh, delicate wine to the rich, full-bodied Hill Country Cellars Chardonnay. They are both delicious but obviously complement foods prepared differently.

Wines can be dry or sweet, fruity or herbaceous, floral or spicy, or some of each. It is easier to look for the larger categories: floral rather than a particular flower, or herbaceous rather than a specific herb. Then reduce it to something more finite, if you like. A single grape variety—Chenin Blanc or Sauvignon Blanc, for instance — may be represented by numerous styles. Sauvignon Blanc can be light-bodied, crisp, floral, and balanced or it can be dry, full-bodied, and herbaceous with good, tart acidity. Knowing the differences among styles helps in selecting the proper wine for a dish. These are learned by tasting and keeping notes.

There are several ways to record your wine impressions. Check the color for clarity and depth of hue; sniff for broadly identified categories, then narrow to more finite ones; check for weight, balance and structure, and then see how long the flavor lasts when you swallow—called a long or short finish. In their book titled *Wine, An Introduction*, Maynard Amerine and Vernon Singleton suggest a scorecard. It lists appearance, color, aroma and bouquet, vinegary, total acidity, sweetness, body, flavor, bitterness and astringency, and general quality. It invites the taster to assign a one or two to each category. A wine scoring seventeen or above is considered good. Professor Ann Noble at the University of California at Davis devised the Wine Aroma Wheel. It begins with ten categories and refines them with definitive words twice more: microbiological refines to lactic, yeasty or other which refines to horsey, lactic acid, sweaty, sauerkraut, and so forth. *Academie du Vin Complete Wine Course* by Stephen Spurrier and Michel Dovaz divides aromas into eight groups: animal, balsamic, empyreumatic, chemical, spicy, floral, fruit, and vegetal/mineral. These terms are then further refined. There are also other types of descriptors and wine evaluations. Pick one that works for you and develop the habit of using it. A greater appreciation and knowledge of wine follows automatically.

I encourage you to trust your own palate and experiment. Organize a wine and cheese tasting with your friends. Select three or four cheeses and three or four wines and try each with the other to learn your preferences. It's a fun and entertaining way to spend the evening. The same sort of taste fest can be centered around wines and meats — a seafood, a poultry selection and veal, for example, or a series of pastas. Tasting is the only way to truly learn. And such informal gatherings can be very pleasant times and a delightful way of sharing. Marcel Proust wrote: "The smell and taste of things remain poised a long time, like souls, ready to remind us." Start creating some fun memories today.

RECIPES

Wine Recipe

*(A recipe of the 1860s from an Austin, Texas,
relative of Liz Carpenter)*

Having gathered your grapes, you will pull them off their bunches (and I believe that you would have a more delicate wine if you were to hull the grapes as the skin possesses a good deal of the tartaric acid together with a mucilaginous property found in the wine prepared from the Mustang grape). Next, put them in a barrel that will not leak, mash and pound them up. Let them there remain till the process of fermentation is complete. The next thing is to get the juice thus obtained from the hulls, and for economy's sake, take a barrel if you are making much, knock the head out, and put it over a stand, cover with hay or straw, and by a lever, press or squeeze all of the juice out, catching it in a trough or anything you may have beneath, or you may strain through a piece of cloth. The idea is to get the juice from the hulls. The next move is the destruction of the excess acid in the juice. You will proceed as follows: get a good tight barrel cleaned well, then burn a rag saturated in sulphur. You put the rag in at the bung, having previously lighted it. Next, cover the bung with something to keep the smoke in. Let it stand for several hours till the fire is burnt out, *but look out or you will get blowed up!* To prevent the explosion before you put in the sulphur rag, wrinse [*sic*] the barrel in cold water.

Then take for every 40 gallons of juice and add to it 1 gallon brandy, 10 pounds sugar, and ½ pint saleratus. Put in the barrel together. In ten days, draw off. Sulphur the barrel again and add more spirit-sugar, . . . if needed.

Respectfully,

Arthur I. Lott (?)

Sweet and Sour Holiday Ham

1 cup celery	1 teaspoon prepared mustard
⅓ cup chopped Bermuda onion	1 tablespoon white wine vinegar
⅓ cup chopped green onion	¼ cup catsup
1 cup chopped sweet bell pepper (red or green)	¼ cup apricot preserves
2 tablespoons butter	2½ cups ham (cooked and diced or sliced)
1½ tablespoons each flour and butter for paste	4 cups rice (cooked)
1 can (12 ounces) apricot nectar	

Sauté onions, bell pepper, and celery in butter on low heat slowly for 5 minutes. Separately, melt second portion of butter and mix in flour for a paste. Add apricot nectar, mustard, wine vinegar, catsup, and preserves, and season with salt and fresh cracked pepper. Add onions, bell pepper, and celery to thickened nectar mixture. Stir until smooth. Add ham and heat thoroughly on low heat for 20 minutes. Serve on rice. If desired, reserve 2 tablespoons each of red bell pepper and celery for garnish. Will serve 5 persons. Choose Gewurztraminer, Chenin Blanc, or a blush wine to complement this dish.

Texas Wine Beef

5 pounds chuck roast	$\frac{1}{2}$ cup parsley (minced)
Lowry's seasoned salt	$2\frac{1}{2}$ cups Texas red wine
Garlic salt	3 bay leaves
$\frac{1}{2}$ pound bacon	1 teaspoon thyme
3 or 4 large carrots (diced)	$\frac{1}{2}$ cups fresh mushrooms
4 cloves garlic (crushed)	(sliced), optional
2 leeks (chopped)	Flour and water for thick-
2 medium onions (chopped)	ening paste

Rub both sides of roast with seasoned salts, and sear. Roast in 350-degree oven for $1\frac{1}{2}$ hours. It should be crusty and well done. Cool and cube. Reserve drippings; add enough water for gravy. Set aside.

Fry bacon, and retain enough grease to cook vegetables. Drain bacon when crisp. Add diced and chopped vegetables to bacon grease and cook slowly, stirring until the carrots look candied.

Place cubed meat in heavy casserole, and cover with the wine. Add bay leaves, thyme and pan drippings. Add cooked vegetables and place in a moderate oven (350 degrees) for about 2 hours. Add bacon and fresh mushrooms (optional) for last few minutes. The sauce should be thick, not watery. Correct with flour paste if necessary.

Serve on wild rice, if available. Makes 6 large or 8 small servings.

Serve Cabernet Sauvignon.

This dish may be prepared a week in advance and frozen.

Potato and Parsley Soup

1 large Bermuda onion	1 or 2 cups Half and Half
3 tablespoons butter	cream
5 medium to large (5-inch)	½ cup parsley
potatoes	Salt and pepper
4 to 5 cups chicken stock	

Slice onion and sauté in skillet with butter until tender but not brown. Add thinly sliced potatoes, and cook covered in chicken stock (instant is fine) until done, 15 minutes or so. Cool. Blend a small portion at a time with cream until it is the consistency you prefer. Add snipped parsley, ½ cup to 3 cups of soup, and blend in blender until thoroughly refined. Season with salt and pepper to taste, and chill. Serve ice cold or hot, with Chardonnay or Chenin Blanc. Garnish with parsley and thin carrot slivers. Serves 6 to 8.

Texas Buttermilk Pie

1 cup sugar	1 cup buttermilk
4 tablespoons flour	1 teaspoon vanilla
⅓ cup melted butter	Dash of nutmeg (optional)
3 eggs, beaten	1 9-inch uncooked pie shell

Preheat oven at 415 degrees. Mix sugar and flour together until fine. Add cooled butter, beaten eggs, buttermilk, and vanilla. Mix and pour into a 9-inch pie crust. Bake 15 minutes at 415 degrees. Turn temperature down to 325 degrees, and continue to bake until the pie sets — about 25 minutes. Cool on rack; do not cut while hot.

(Recipe by Carolyn Heinzelmann)

Fall Creek Kingfish With Apples and Mustard

1½ pounds Kingfish mackerel filets (Maimai may be substituted)

6 tablespoons cumin	⇨ Fill shaker with 3 to 1
2 tablespoons cinnamon	ratio of seasonings

3 tablespoons butter
6 lady apples (peeled, cored and sliced)
6 tablespoons currants
3 tablespoons coarse, mild mustard
½ cup cream
½ cup chopped, toasted pecans

Coat fish filets with olive oil and dust filets with cumin/cinnamon mixture. Grill 3–4 minutes each side. Be careful not to overcook and dry out fish. Remove from grill; cover and keep warm.

To make sauce:

Sauté 6 lady apples in 3 tablespoons butter. Add 6 tablespoons currants. After apple slices are slightly browned, add 3 tablespoons mustard and ½ cup cream. Mix and heat thoroughly. Correct seasoning.

Pour sauce over filets and sprinkle with toasted chopped pecans.

Serve Fall Creek Chardonnay, Sauvignon Blanc, and Emerald Riesling.

Château Montgolfier Mexican Salad

1 pound ground beef	1 cup grated Cheddar cheese
½ teaspoon salt	1 cup Italian or French salad
1 medium onion (chopped)	dressing
1 can Ranch Style Beans (drained)	1 package tortilla chips (crushed)
1 head lettuce	1 large avocado (sliced)
4 tomatoes, cut in wedges	Hot sauce

Brown beef in skillet; add salt, onion, and beans. Simmer 10 minutes. Combine all ingredients and top with the avocado. Serve with hot sauce and a Rosé.

Fall Creek
Wild Rice and Pecan Stuffing for Wild Turkey

1 cup wild rice	½ cup butter
1 cup water	¼ cup chopped onion
1 cup chicken broth	½ cup sliced mushrooms
1 tablespoon butter	½ cup raisins
½ teaspoon salt	¼ cup minced bacon
¼ teaspoon black pepper	½ cup chopped pecans

Cook wild rice in top of double boiler with 1 cup water, 1 cup chicken broth, 1 tablespoon butter, ½ teaspoon salt, and ¼ teaspoon pepper.

Melt ½ cup butter in a skillet. Sauté chopped onions until golden; then add mushrooms and raisins and cook until tender. Add content of skillet along with bacon and pecans to wild rice. Serve with Fall Creek Chardonnay.

Fall Creek Cracker Crumb Bass

Fresh bass or perch	1	cup saltine crackers, rolled to fine crumbs
Flour		
Cavender's All-Purpose Greek Seasoning	3	eggs
	$\frac{1}{2}$	cup Half and Half
	$\frac{1}{2}$	cup unsalted butter

Have your favorite fisherman filet those freshly caught bass or perch. Filets should be checked carefully to remove any small bones. Season filets with Greek Seasoning on both sides. Shake filets in flour, then dip floured filets into eggs beaten with Half and Half; roll filets in cracker crumbs until coated well. Let coated filets sit for 15 minutes before placing in skillet of hot melted butter. Season with salt and pepper. Cook 6–8 minutes on each side. Serve immediately with Fall Creek Sauvignon Blanc or Chardonnay.

Cypress Valley Dry Venison Sausage

8	pounds pork fat	1	teaspoon red pepper
30	pounds venison	2	teaspoons diced red pepper
$1\frac{1}{2}$	teaspoons salt peter		
6	tablespoons black pepper	2	teaspoons chili powder
$1\frac{1}{2}$	teaspoons sage	$2\frac{1}{2}$	teaspoons paprika
5	teaspoons garlic powder		

Grind the pork fat (or bacon ends) and venison to desired consistency. Blend seasonings together, then add to meat mixture. Stuff into casings (pork is preferable to beef casings). Smoke and dry as per your preference. Smoking is a fine art, so you may wish to have the old fellow down the road do what he is best at (or better than you, anyway!). Serve with Cabernet Sauvignon.

Cypress Valley Venison Stroganoff

1 **pound venison backstrap butterfly steaks***	2 **cloves garlic (minced)**
	½ **cup mushrooms (sliced)**
2 **cups red wine or buttermilk**	1 **medium onion (sliced)**
½ **cup flour**	1 **can (8 oz.) consommé**
½ **teaspoon salt**	¼ **cup water**
¼ **teaspoon freshly ground pepper**	1 **cup sour cream**
	¼ **cup dry sherry (optional)**
¼ **pound butter**	

Marinate venison in red wine or buttermilk overnight. Combine flour, salt, and pepper. Rub venison with garlic. Slice venison crosswise against the grain into thin ¼-inch slices. Toss in flour mixture.

Sauté mushrooms and onions until golden in ⅛ pound butter. Remove from pan into bowl. Add remainder of butter to pan and heat well (do not brown). Add venison and cook for 5 minutes. The meat should still be a bit red and sticky.

Return mushrooms and onions to pan.

Add consommé and water. Cook uncovered in skillet over low heat for 1½ hours. Just prior to serving, add sour cream and sherry. Serve over egg noodles or Rösti with Cabernet Sauvignon. Serves 4–6 people.

* During deer harvest, take backstrap from young doe, prepare and freeze it for later use as follows. To butterfly the backstrap, cut 1-inch slices crosswise across the backstrap, them make a third cut halfway through the entire thickness. Pound the steak outward from this cut (essentially looks like a butterfly). Wrap well and freeze.

Quail a la Buena Vida

8 **quail (stuffed with apple slices)**	2 **carrots, diced**
	1 **cup chopped celery**
1¼ **cups butter**	1 **teaspoon fine herbs**
½ **cup chicken broth**	2 **tomatoes (diced)**
¾ **cup La Buena Vida Vineyards Vidal Blanc**	1 **can (15 oz.) celery hearts (drained)**
4 **large shallots, minced**	

Heat butter in large skillet or roasting pan and brown quail on all sides. Add chicken broth, Vidal Blanc wine, shallots, carrots, celery, herbs, and tomatoes. Cover tightly and simmer 1 hour or until tender. Remove lid and add celery hearts. Heat until piping hot, about 5 minutes. Place quail and celery hearts on serving platter and spoon pan juices over quail. If desired, the pan juices may be thickened with mixture of $\frac{1}{4}$ cup flour and $\frac{1}{2}$ cup chicken broth. Makes about 4 servings.

Serve with crusty French bread and La Buena Vida Vineyards Texas Gold.

This recipe can also be used for game hens (larger) with optional stuffing.

Stuffing (optional – for 6 larger game hens):

In bowl mix 12 crisp rusks (biscuits), crumbled, $\frac{1}{4}$ cup melted butter, 1 can (15$\frac{1}{2}$ oz.) whole natural chestnuts, drained and crumbled, 1 cup chicken broth, $\frac{1}{2}$ apple, minced, 1 egg. Season to taste with salt and use mixture to stuff hens. Cook and serve as for Quail a la Buena Vida.

Venison a la Buena Vida

Venison (leg, roast or . . .	3 onions (quartered)
can substitute lamb or	1 green pepper (cubed)
kid)	1 cup canned mushrooms
Salt and pepper	1 small jar sliced pimientos
2 cups La Buena Vida Vine-	1 lemon (sliced)
yards Blanc de Noir	1 teaspoon dried tarragon
2 cans (8 oz.) tomato sauce	2 bay leaves
1 can consommé	$\frac{1}{4}$ teaspoon dried thyme
2 teaspoons tarragon vinegar	6 leaves of rosemary

Remove all skin and fat from the venison. Sprinkle with salt and pepper. Place in roaster. Combine Blanc de Noir with tomato sauce and consommé. Add vinegar, onions, peppers, mushrooms, pimientos, lemon, and seasonings. Pour over venison. Marinate in this for 2 to 3 days in the refrigerator. When ready to roast, put a rack under the meat, leaving the sauce around it. Brown quickly in a hot oven (400), cover and roast slowly (300), basting frequently for about 3 hours or until meat is tender.

Serve with La Buena Vida Vineyards Blanc de Noir.

Messina Hof Apples in Dressing Gowns
(Apple Dumplings)

³⁄₄ cup finely chopped dates	2 egg whites
³⁄₄ cup finely chopped pecans	1 teaspoon sugar
½ cup brandy	¼ cup finely chopped pecans
4 apples, peeled and cored	1 cup whipping cream
Cinnamon	3 tablespoons brandy
4 tablespoons sugar	2 tablespoons sugar
Pie crust dough for two pie shells	

Soak chopped dates and pecans in brandy overnight.

Sprinkle apples with cinnamon, stuff with date-nut mixture, and place in a small, non-stick baking pan. Pour in ½ inch of water. Top each apple with 1 tablespoon sugar and bake in a 350-degree oven until tender (about 40 minutes), maintaining ½ inch of water in bottom of pan. Let apples cool slightly and remove from baking dish.

Divide pie dough into quarters and roll out thinly. Wrap each apple and place on a parchment paper-lined baking sheet.

Beat egg whites until frothy; add 1 teaspoon of sugar and beat until softly peaking. Cover dough-wrapped apples with the meringue and sprinkle with ¼ cup chopped pecans. Bake in a 400-degree oven until light golden brown, about 15–20 minutes.

Beat whipping cream with brandy and sugar to soft peaks. Top dumplings with whipped cream and serve individually with Messina Hof Late Harvest Johannisberg Riesling.

Messina Hof Fettuccine Messina

Toss cooked fettuccine with Vino Di Amore Sweet Bianco wine that has been warmed to room temperature. Top with a cream sauce of butter, Romano cheese, and cream. Serve with the German-style Vino Di Amore Sweet Bianco, which nicely balances the richness of the pasta.

Messina Hof Lamb Chops Marinara

4	lamb chops, from roasted rack of lamb	1	teaspoon minced parsley
		½	onion, minced
4	tomatoes, finely chopped	2	tablespoons olive oil
1	teaspoon crushed oregano		Salt and pepper to taste

Arrange lamb chops in a shallow baking dish. Mix tomatoes, oregano, parsley, onion, and olive oil; spread over meat and sprinkle with salt and pepper. Broil until sauce is warm. Serve with warm French bread and butter, and Messina Hof Cabernet.

Ste. Genevieve Pollo Carbon

2	8-ounce boneless chicken breasts or 1 small white chicken	1	tablespoon fajita spice
		1	large garlic clove, chopped
			Juice of ½ lime
1	pint Italian dressing		

Remove skin and rub chicken with chopped garlic. Put chicken in a small bowl and cover with Italian dressing and lime juice. Refrigerate for 24 hours. Before cooking, season chicken with fajita spice. Charcoal broil with mesquite charcoal until well done. Before serving top chicken breast, or slices of whole chicken, with ½-inch thickness of Tomatillo Butter. Serves 2. Serve with Ste. Genevieve French Colombard.

Tomatillo Butter:

¼	pound tomatillo, peeled and halved	1	cup chicken stock
		¼	tablespoon fresh garlic, chopped
¼	pound anaheim peppers, stems removed	1¼	pounds butter

In very hot skillet, char tomatillos and peppers until black. Add tomatillos and peppers to chicken stock with garlic. Salt and pepper to taste. Cover and simmer for 30 minutes. Put through meat grinder with medium holes (or coarsely chop) and let cool. Take 1¼ pounds of butter and mix in a bowl until soft. Blend with tomatillo/pepper mixture. Place on wax paper and roll up jelly-roll fashion, about the size of a silver dollar. Chill until firm.

Ste. Genevieve
Rose of Cabernet Sea Scallops

1½	pounds sea scallops	1	tablespoon pink pepper-
1	large tomato, peeled,		corns
	seeded, chopped	¼	cup opal basil (fresh)
½	cup leeks, sliced		julienned
3	shallots, minced		Salt to taste
2	cloves garlic, minced		Freshly ground white
2	tablespoons clarified		pepper, to taste
	butter		Flour for dredging
¼	cup Rose of Cabernet	2	tablespoons cream

Season scallops with salt and pepper and dredge in flour. Place clarified butter in a sauté pan and heat until very hot. Add scallops and sauté until cooked through and golden. Remove scallops to a warm plate. To sauté pan, add shallots, garlic, leeks, tomato, and pink peppercorns. Sauté for 30 seconds. Deglaze ingredients with Rose of Cabernet, add cream and cook for about 15 seconds. Pour sauce over scallops and serve immediately. Serves 4.

Ste. Genevieve West Texas Quail

8	quail (4 Cornish hens)	1	small zucchini, chopped
1	large tomato, peeled,	1	small yellow squash,
	seeded, chopped		chopped
¼	cup red onion, chopped		Juice and zest of 1 lime
2	small or 1 large jalapeño,		Salt to taste
	minced	1	tablespoon cracked black
6	corn tortillas, cut in strips		pepper

Rinse quail and pat dry. Salt and pepper each quail inside and outside. Combine all other ingredients. Adjust seasoning. Stuff quail with tortilla mixture. Tie legs. Place quail in roasting pan. Brush with butter or oil. Roast in 375-degree oven for approximately 5–7 minutes or until done. Serves 4.

Roasted Mallard Duck

2 small mallards or one 5-pound duckling	6 apples (peeled and quartered)
Salt and cracked pepper	1 tablespoon sugar
4 tablespoons butter	$\frac{1}{2}$ teaspoon salt
	$\frac{1}{4}$ teaspoon cinnamon
Stuffing:	$\frac{1}{4}$ teaspoon sage
	3 tablespoons cognac
$\frac{3}{4}$ pound sausage meat	$\frac{1}{3}$ cup beef consommé
Duck giblets	$\frac{1}{3}$ cup Texas port wine

Brown sausage in skillet and pour off most of fat. Sauté chopped giblets with sausage and remove to bowl. Sauté apples until slightly brown but still firm. Remove to bowl and sprinkle with sugar, cinnamon, salt, sage, and cover with cognac.

Cook consommé and wine to reduce to $\frac{1}{4}$ cup. Pour into sausage and giblet bowl and mix. Toss in apples and stuff mallards loosely with the stuffing.

Salt and pepper and butter the mallards all over. Roast them in a 375-degree preheated oven until browned. Reduce heat to 325 degrees and cook until done, usually $1\frac{1}{2}$ hours. (The larger duckling takes $2\frac{1}{2}$ hours.) Baste ducks with pan juices often. Cover with sauce and serve. Serves 4.

Texas Port Wine Sauce:

Simmer 2 cups consommé and 1 cup port until reduced to $1\frac{1}{4}$ cups. Add 4 tablespoons butter and serve with a Texas red wine.

Texas Wine Pheasant

3 pheasant ($1\frac{1}{2}$ to 2 pounds)	3 pieces bacon
Salt and cracked pepper and butter (soft)	$1\frac{1}{2}$ cups white Texas wine (dry)
3 cloves garlic	3 tablespoons chopped red onion
3 whole sweet cloves	
3 tablespoons chopped parsley	1 cup instant chicken bouillon
3 tablespoons chopped celery (with leaves)	$\frac{1}{4}$ teaspoon salt
3 thinly sliced pieces of lemon	$\frac{1}{4}$ cup fresh, sliced mushrooms

Rub pheasants inside and out with salt and pepper and butter. Place garlic, parsley, celery, lemon slice, and clove inside each bird and sprinkle with white Texas wine. Cover each bird with a bacon strip and roast them in a moderate oven (375 degrees) for approximately 45 minutes.

Baste frequently with following sauce: Combine red onion, bouillon, wine, and mushrooms (salt if needed) and cook to reduce. Strain pan juices and serve as gravy. Serves 6.

Rabbit Casserole

$4\frac{1}{2}$	to 5-pound rabbit	3	tablespoons parsley
3	cups red wine (dry)	3	tablespoons celery
$\frac{1}{2}$	cup bacon grease ($\frac{1}{8}$ teaspoon salt)	3	cloves garlic
		1	teaspoon salt
3	tablespoons flour	$\frac{1}{4}$	teaspoon cracked pepper
2	cups water	30	pearl onions
1	tablespoon tomato purée	$\frac{1}{2}$	cup heavy cream

Cut rabbit into serving pieces and marinate for 2 days in the red wine. Drain and dry well and reserve the marinade.

Heat bacon grease and salt in casserole on top of range. Drench rabbit in flour, and brown all sides in casserole. Add wine marinade, water, tomato purée, parsley, celery, garlic, salt, and pepper. Cover; bring to boil and simmer 25 minutes. Brown onions in bacon grease and add to casserole. Simmer for 45 minutes more. Add mushrooms and simmer another 25 minutes. When rabbit is tender and done, stir in the cream, correct the seasoning, and simmer 5 minutes more. Serves 6. Serve with a dry, medium-bodied Texas red wine.

Turkey Croquettes

3	tablespoons bacon grease	1	cup scalded Half and Half
3	tablespoons onion		cream
	(chopped)	2	egg yolks
5	tablespoons Texas port,	$\frac{1}{4}$	cup Half and Half cream
	plus 1 tablespoon water	$\frac{1}{3}$	cup grated Gruyère
$1\frac{2}{3}$	cup diced, cooked turkey		Salt and cracked pepper
$\frac{1}{2}$	teaspoon oregano	2	eggs
3	tablespoons butter	2	tablespoons vegetable oil
3	tablespoons flour		Flour and breadcrumbs to
			coat croquettes

Sauté onion in bacon grease. Add port and simmer until liquid equals 2 tablespoons. Add turkey and oregano. Mix. Set aside.

Make roux with butter and flour (3 tablespoons each) and slowly add scalded cream to make a smooth, thick white sauce.

Beat 2 egg yolks with cream and slowly stir into the white sauce. Remove from heat. Add turkey, cheese, salt, and cracked pepper to taste. Chill $1\frac{1}{2}$ to 2 hours.

Shape into desired size (recipe makes 25 croquettes) and chill.

Beat eggs with 2 tablespoons vegetable oil. Prepare plate of flour and a plate of breadcrumbs. Roll croquette in flour, then in egg-oil mixture (cover croquette completely), then in breadcrumbs. Chill in refrigerator 1 hour. Repeat.

Heat enough vegetable oil (375 degrees) to reach $1\frac{1}{2}$ inches high in skillet. Fry several croquettes until brown. Drain on paper and keep warm in oven. Repeat until all croquettes are fried and serve with your favorite Texas wine. Serves 6.

Wimberley Valley Wild Game Shish Kebob

½ pound venison, ½ pound   2   each of red, green, and
   dove, ½ pound quail   yellow peppers
1 bottle WVW Cabernet Blanc   Red and black pepper
   or WVW Chenin Blanc   Garlic powder
   or Bar-B-Que wine   1   large container mushrooms
2 large sweet onions   Cumin

Marinade:

½ cup lemon juice   1   cup Bar-B-Que wine

Debone and cube meat into 1-inch cubes. Marinate in marinade and then lightly dust meat with cumin, garlic powder, and red and black pepper. Add water to marinade-covered meat, allow to sit 4 to 6 hours. Cut onions and bell peppers into slices comparable to meat. Skewer mushrooms whole and alternate meat and vegetables. Use a hot fire and grill 5 to 7 minutes on each side. Accompany with suggested wines. Serves 4 to 6 adults.

Optional sauce:

1 cup honey, ½ cup Cabernet Sauvignon, ½ cup lemon juice, 1 teaspoon finely chopped jalapeño peppers. Warm to slow boil and then brush on kebobs.

Texas Veal with Red Wine

1 cup red wine   ¼ cup wild mushrooms, sliced
¼ cup shallots, chopped   1   pound thinly sliced veal, cut
¼ cup onions, chopped   in four pieces
3 cups brown gravy   2   tablespoons flour
   (homemade, canned,   2   tablespoons butter
   or from a mix)   Salt and pepper

Combine first three ingredients in a medium saucepan over high heat and reduce to ⅔ cup. Lower heat and add gravy. Mix together well and strain. Reserve and keep warm.

Pound veal steaks to desired thinness and dredge in flour seasoned with salt and pepper. Heat butter in large skillet and sauté veal over medium heat about 3 minutes. Turn veal and add mushrooms. Cook 3 more minutes. Serve immediately with sauce and your favorite Texas wine. Makes 4 servings.

FOOD/WINE LIST

Barbeque: Cabernet Sauvignon, Zinfandel
Beans and Corn Bread: Zinfandel, Chenin Blanc
Chalupas with Avocado: Chenin Blanc, sparkling wines,
    Chardonnay
Chicken (grilled): Chenin Blanc, blush wines; **(spicier dishes):**
    Chardonnay, Sauvignon Blanc
Chili: Riesling, Zinfandel, sparkling wines
Curried Foods: Gewurztraminer, sparkling wines, Chenin Blanc
Enchiladas: blush wines, sparkling wines, Texas whites
Ham: Gewurztraminer, Chenin Blanc, Chardonnay, Riesling
Lamb: Cabernet Sauvignon, Texas reds, Pinot Noir
Mushrooms Stuffed with Herbs: Chenin Blanc, Sauvignon
    Blanc, Gewurztraminer
Pasta with Cream: Chardonnay, Pinot Noir
Pasta with Seafood: Chardonnay or Sauvignon Blanc
Pasta with Meat Sauce: Zinfandel, Merlot, Texas reds
Pasta Salad: blush wines, Riesling, Chenin Blanc, sparkling
    wines
Peanut Butter Sandwich: sparkling wines
Rabbit: blush wines, Chardonnay, Texas whites
Grilled or Roasted Beef: Cabernet Sauvignon, Merlot
Redfish: Chardonnay, Sauvignon Blanc
Shrimp: Sauvignon Blanc, Chardonnay, sparkling wines
Soups (hearty): Texas reds
Steaks: Cabernet Sauvignon, Merlot
Turkey: Chenin Blanc, Chardonnay, Texas whites and reds,
    Zinfandel
Venison: Cabernet Sauvignon, Merlot, Chardonnay

CHEESE/WINE LIST

Appenzeller: Chenin Blanc, Riesling, Gewurztraminer,
    Chardonnay
Blue Cheese: Zinfandel, Cabernet Sauvignon, sparkling wines,
    Muscat Canelli, port
Brie, Camembert, Coulommiers, Rouy: Cabernet Sauvignon,
    Zinfandel, sparkling wines, Sauvignon Blanc, Chardonnay
Cantal: Sauvignon Blanc, Barbera
Cheddars: (mild) Chenin Blanc, Cabernet Sauvignon; (sharp)
    Chardonnay

Doux de Montagne: Chardonnay, Riesling, sparkling wines
Edam: Cabernet Sauvignon, Merlot, Zinfandel
Emmenthaler: Sauvignon Blanc, Chardonnay, Cabernet
  Sauvignon, Zinfandel, sparkling wines, Riesling
Feta: Chenin Blanc, blush wines, proprietary wines
Fontina (French Fontal): Cabernet Franc, Cabernet Sauvignon,
  Barbera, Riesling, blush wines
Goat Cheese: Sauvignon Blanc, blush wines, Texas whites
Gouda: Chenin Blanc, Riesling, sparkling wines; **Aged Gouda:**
  Chardonnay, Cabernet Sauvignon, Zinfandel
Havarti: Barbera, Zinfandel, Riesling, blush wines
Jarlsberg: Ruby Cabernet, proprietary reds, Riesling
Monterey Jack: suits most wines; Chenin Blanc, Chardonnay,
  Riesling, proprietary wines, blush wines, Cabernet
  Sauvignon, Zinfandel
Mozzarella: Chenin Blanc, Chardonnay, Barbera, Sauvignon
  Blanc
Muenster (domestic): Sauvignon Blanc, blush wines
Munster (Alsatian): Gewurztraminer
Pont l'Eveque: Cabernet Sauvignon, Zinfandel
Port Salut: Chenin Blanc, Riesling, blush wines, proprietary
  wines
Provolone: Cabernet Sauvignon, Zinfandel, Chenin Blanc, blush
  wines
Reblochon: Cabernet Sauvignon, Merlot, sparkling wines
Revidoux: blush wines, Cabernet Sauvignon, Chardonnay,
  sparkling wines
Sonoma Dry Jack: Cabernet Sauvignon, Barbera, Zinfandel
St. André: Riesling, sparkling wines, Cabernet Sauvignon
Tilsit: Zinfandel, Barbera, Cabernet Sauvignon

[Cheese and lettuce served together for the salad course is becoming increasingly popular. Blue cheeses and mild goat cheeses are often used and complemented by toasted walnuts and pecans.]

Appendix

Wine cheers the sad,
Revives the old,
And inspires the young.

— George Gordon, Lord Byron

HISTORY OF THE NEW
TEXAS WINE GRAPE INDUSTRY

George Ray McEachern
Extension Hortuculturist
Texas A&M University
College Station, Texas 77843

February 2, 1995

Grapes grow naturally in Texas. Thirteen of the twenty-six species which grow around the world were described as native to Texas by the legendary T. V. Munson of Denison, Texas, in 1909.

Prior to prohibition, there were at least sixteen commercial wineries operating in Texas. Only Val Verde Winery in Del Rio, Texas, was reestablished after prohibition and continues to operate today.

Interest in commercial grape culture was essentially nonexistent until the national wine revolution of the late 1960s. In the early 1970s vineyards were planted in every state of the nation. Texans likewise began to experiment with small vineyards across the state. The first plantings in the early 1970s to eventually grow into commercial wineries were planted by Clint McPherson of Lubbock, Texas, and Bobby Smith of Arlington, Texas.

NATURAL FACTORS WHICH LIMIT COMMERCIAL GRAPE CULTURE IN TEXAS

Grape culture in Texas is not without problems, otherwise an industry would have existed before today. Production has become limited to those areas of the state which are not significantly affected by the following limiting factors.

Pierce's Disease, long recognized as "the" significant limiting factor for grape culture in the Gulf Coast States, is a major negative force in Texas. It is most widespread south of the 800 hour winter chilling line. Numerous vineyards in East and South Texas have experienced complete loss from PD since 1970. Isolated vineyards in the West Cross Timbers and Hill Country are infected. Tolerant varieties and muscadines are currently the only control of PD east of I-35 and south of US 290. LeNoir, Favorite, and Blanc du Bois are the best PD resistant wine varieties for East and South Texas.

Cotton Root Rot is a significant problem in areas of the state which have high pH alkaline soils. It is not a problem in the acid soils of East Texas or in the soils on the South Plains near Lubbock, Texas. Texas needs a rootstock for Cotton Root Rot control. Limited progress has been made with *Vitis Andicans* propagation for this purpose.

Hail is a problem in many of the better grape producing areas of North, Central, and West Texas. Vines can be stripped of bark and foliage by a hail storm of only a few minutes.

Winter Freezes are a major problem in Texas. The Texas wine industry prospered for fourteen years before a freeze in late October with temperatures dropping sixty degrees in twenty-four hours killed hundreds of acres of mature grapevines in 1989 and again in 1993. The *Vitis vinifera* grape is grown in very cold climates; however, the grape does not have a true dormancy or rest period. Consequently, vines can have cell activity during warm periods of the fall or winter, which preconditions the vine for freeze injury. In addition, spring frosts can kill new growth. Young *Vitis vinifera* vine establishment can be difficult in West Texas due to early fall freezes. Freezes pose a serious problem for grafted vines, because rootstock vines are extremely difficult to redevelop into a new trunk following a damaging freeze.

Grape Root Phylloxera devastated the vineyards of Europe in the 1880s and it has recently necessitated the replanting of the vineyards of Napa and Sonoma. Grape Root Phylloxera has been confirmed to infest a vineyard in Texas, and every effort will need to be exercised to prevent its spread.

Fungus Diseases, particularly Black Rot, are serious problems in Texas and make the use of fungicides obligatory. Without effective fungicides, *Vitis vinifera* varieties cannot be grown in much of Texas.

Crown Gall has seriously reduced the production of vineyards in every region of the state. Cultivation, hail, and freeze damage is frequently followed by Crown Gall.

Other natural limiting factors are water volume, water quality, insects, predators such as deer, raccoons, birds, and weeds. Additional factors influencing the Texas wine grape industry include financing, marketing, laws, vineyard technology, enology technology, equipment supply, labor, and others.

Types of Grapes Evaluated in Texas

As the Texas industry developed, four basic types of grapes were planted:

1. American Grapes such as Champanel
2. *Vinifera* Grapes such as Chenin Blanc
3. Hybrid Grapes such as Villard Blanc
4. Muscadine Grapes such as Scuppernong

American grapes have a high degree of cold tolerance and disease resistance but are generally considered to make a poorer quality of wine than *vinifera* grapes. Less than 100 acres of American grapes are grown commercially in Texas. Early planting in East and South Texas were of the American type, such as Black Spanish.

Vinifera **grapes** are the true wine grapes of Europe and exhibit high yields of grapes which make quality wines. They cannot be grown in South or East Texas because of PD and

freeze susceptibility. In the last five years, Texas grape growers have learned that the *vinifera* type grapes will perform
well in Texas. It was this discovery that stimulated the almost revolutionary expansion of the new industry. Commercial attempts to grow *vinifera* grape at Crystal City by
O. P. Leonard and at Rio Grande City by A. V. Peterson met
with failure. In addition, *vinifera* planted in East and South
Texas were killed by PD. Consequently, the success with *vinifera* grapes at Lubbock, Bakersfield, Springtown, and Tow
in the late 1970s stimulated great interest in potential for
commercial wine grape production. These grapes have
proven to be outstanding in Central, West, and North
Texas. *Vinifera* grape culture and top quality *vinifera* wines
are the major reason the Texas wine grape industry has continued to grow and prosper.

Hybrid grapes are intermediate, demonstrating the
cold hardiness and disease resistance of the American par-
ents plus the production and quality of *vinifera*. The first
vineyards of the new Texas industry were of the hybrid type
varieties. Of these Villard Blanc, Vidal Blanc, Chambourcin,
Aurelia, Rayon d'Or, Chancellor, and Verdelet performed
well. Good to very good wine has been made from most of
these varieties. These grapes are becoming less popular due
to the performance of the *vinifera* grapes.

Muscadines are not considered true bunch grapes.
They are grown in the acid soils of East Texas.

Types of Grapes Grown in Texas

The Texas wine industry is primarily from the *Vitis vinifera* grape. In the early 1970s French/American hybrid
grapes were planted; however, all but one of these have
been abandoned or converted to *Vitis vinifera*. LeNoir and
Favorite are outstanding Port wine varieties which are in
both South and East Texas where PD prohibits other varieties. Muscadines are grown to a limited extent in East Texas,
with Piney Woods Winery making muscadine wine.

The major *Vitis vinifera* varieties of Europe can be
grown effectively in North, Central, and West Texas. Cabernet Sauvignon is producing quality fruit on the South Plains
south of Lubbock, in the Cross Timbers and Hill Country.

Chardonnay is likewise producing quality fruit and wine in the same areas but also north of Lubbock. Sauvignon Blanc is being produced and made into quality wine from fruit in all areas of West and North Texas. Chenin Blanc produces both high yields and quality fruit from Lubbock to Fort Stockton. The "new" variety in Texas is Merlot, and many other varieties are grown with good success.

MAJOR GRAPE AREAS IN TEXAS

Since 1970, the new grape industry has expanded across the state with close to 1,000 family vineyards being planted. In 1995, there are 300 productive vineyards. Success or failure can depend on many things; however, the proper site, soil, and climate are very important.

South Plains and the Lubbock area has developed into the main grape-producing area of Texas and has approximately 1,300 acres of grapes. The question is how far north can a variety be grown without serious freeze injury. The 0°F average annual minimum temperature line is the upper limit for *Vitis vinifera* culture. White Riesling and Chardonnay are grown north to Plainview and Sauvignon Blanc and Zinfandel slightly north of Lubbock. Cabernet Sauvignon, Muscat Canelli, and Chenin Blanc need to be grown south of Lubbock. With time, each variety will find its specific site on the South Plains. The advantages of the area include a very dry climate, deep well-drained fertile soil, sufficient water, cool nights during the growing season, no Cotton Root Rot, no Pierce's Disease, and a strong agricultural community. The wineries in Central Texas depend heavily upon grapes produced on the South Plains.

Far West Texas also has large grape acreage, with approximately 1,200 acres. Though vineyards have been established at Van Horn, Dell City, Midland, El Paso, Fort Davis, and Valentine, the dominant vineyard in Texas is the 1,000-acre Ste. Genevieve Vineyard twenty miles east of Fort Stockton. In West Texas, the *vinifera* grape is used exclusively. Chenin Blanc, Sauvignon Blanc, and Chardonnay produce extremely well with yields as high as seven tons per acre. Early fall freezes, iron chlorides, Cotton Root Rot, water supply and water quality are limiting factors. Dry climate, fertile soil, and mild winters are positive for the area. Very good production, vine growth, and wine quality have exceeded expectations. The Davis Mountains of Far West Texas have several outstanding vineyards.

West Cross Timbers of North Central Texas, with 220 acres, has experienced a large number of small commercial vineyards and wineries. The area has excellent horticulture soil, a dry climate, and the advantage of a large metro population base to market their wine. *Vinifera* grapes have produced very well in the area. Vineyards are located in Springtown, Weatherford, Granbury, Ivanhoe, Denison, Montague, and Arlington. The city of Grapevine in 1994 obtained favorable legislation for wineries and plans are under way for their development.

Hill Country area north of Fredericksburg to San Saba and west to Junction is home of the beautiful limestone hills and pristine creeks, with 300 acres of vineyards. The Hill Country is famous for peach production with excellent soil and climate and a natural area for quality vineyards. A large tourist trade and favorable wine laws have encouraged Hill Country vineyards and wineries. Fruit and foliage diseases, hail, and cotton root rot are problems in the area.

East and South Texas has the disadvantage of Pierce's Disease and Black Rot and cannot grow *vinifera* varieties. Val Verde Winery at Del Rio and Messina Hof at Bryan are producing outstanding Port wines from the LeNoir grape, which is resistant to Pierce's Disease. Muscadine wine is made at Piney Woods Winery.

AGENCIES SUPPORTING THE TEXAS GRAPE INDUSTRY

Texas A&M University System, through grower education by the Extension Service and research by the Experiment Station, has played a major role in supporting the industry. Extension and research literature has been published to assist the industry. Teaching in the College of Agriculture has produced both BS and MS students who are leaders in the industry.

Grayson County College teaches a two-year degree and a continuing education program for the industry. The college is home for the T. V. Munson Viticulture and

Enology Center, which has accumulated many of the Munson varieties and makes them available to the public.

Texas Tech University and the Texas Wine Marketing Research Institute supports the industry through evaluating the economic progress and impact of Texas wine on the Texas economy. The Horticulture program has a research vineyard at Brownfield, Texas, and teaches viticulture at the university.

The University of Texas Department of Lands has a research vineyard at Bakersfield, Texas, and a wine laboratory at Midland, Texas. The University of Texas program has introduced FerCal rootstock into the United States from France and has certified vines for sale.

The Texas Department of Agriculture has supported the industry through promotion, legislative guidance, news releases, pest management, and the Lone Star Wine Competition.

The Texas Wine and Grape Growers Association, founded in 1977, conducts at least two educational meetings annually and provides leadership for legislation to improve the industry. They publish a newsletter for their membership and six regional directors coordinate meetings in their regions to assist grape growers and wine makers.

AWARDING TEXAS WINE QUALITY

Three major wine competitions are conducted annually in the state for evaluating and showcasing the high quality of Texas wine. The **Lone Star Wine Competition** is conducted at the State Fair by the TWGGA, TDA, and Texas A&M University. The Houston Club conducts the **Best of Texas Wine Awards and Tasting** each year. The Texas Restaurant Association conducts the **Texas Wine Classic** at their annual meeting.

Texas wines have shown well in the leading competition in California as well as New York, Chicago, Atlanta, and Dallas. Tastings in London, Burgundy, and Bordeaux have demonstrated that Texas wine can be as good as any in the world.

The quality of Texas wine has grown dramatically as

vines become older, vineyard management becomes standardized, and as wine makers improve their skills.

WINERIES

The establishment of wineries followed the vineyards. Production increased from 6,300 gallons in 1975 to 450,500 gallons in 1987. The 1987 crop was frozen across Texas except on the High Plains; consequently, wine production was down in 1987. The future for wineries in Texas is excellent. Excluding Ste. Genevieve, there is a gross overplanting of grapes. The 1988 crop could be larger than the tank capacity currently in Texas. If the current acreage continues to increase, the number of wineries must increase, or the price paid for grapes will fall below a realistic level.

TABLE I. Texas Grape Acreage Estimates in March 1988.

Area	Region	1973	1983	1985	1988
Plains	1	5	933	1,200	2,000
North Central	2	15	369	400	500
East	3	10	71	100	150
Far West	4	20	1,449	1,500	1,200
Hill Country	5	10	112	400	700
South	6	30	66	100	100
TOTALS		**90**	**3,000**	**3,700**	**4,650**

INDUSTRY SUPPORT

Texas Department of Agriculture: Former Commissioner Jim Hightower and Danny Presnal played a major role in promoting the new Texas wine industry beginning in 1983. They conducted numerous tastings across the state and nation and sponsored the Lone Star Wine Competition in cooperation with the TGGA and Southwest Airlines. They have given excellent leadership in supporting legislation for the industry. Commissioner Rick Perry continues the trend.

Texas A&M University: The university established research vineyards at College Station, Montague, and Crystal City from as early as 1880; however, the program was discontinued in 1960 due to low interest in home table and jelly grapes. Researchers Ernest Mortensen and Uiel Randolph were important early grape scientists in Texas. In the early 1970s, Ron Perry established major grape research vineyards at Lubbock, Junction, El Paso, Overton, and Uvalde to evaluate cultivar and rootstock performance. Today, Dr. William N. Lipe coordinates the Texas Agricultural Experiment Station grape research program from the Research Center at Lubbock. As a full-time grape scientist, Dr. Lipe is evaluating cultivars, rootstocks, and cultural systems for improving the Texas grape industry. The Texas Agricultural Extension Service has assisted grape growers in solving production problems since the turn of the century. With the rebirth of the industry in the early 1970s, numerous extension specialists and county extension agents have helped growers throughout the state. In 1974, twenty grape variety trail demonstrations were established with cooperation throughout the state. Between 1975 and 1977, leadership was provided for the formation of the TGGA. George Ray McEachern served as secretary of the association from 1977 through 1984. In 1983, the Extension Service published two bulletins, *Growing Grapes in Texas* and *Texas Vineyard Guide* to assist new growers. In 1986, the Texas Vineyard Management Shortcourse was initiated at College Station. Today all of the authors in this handbook are providing assistance to Texas grape growers.

Texas Tech University: Clinton McPherson, Robert Reed, and Roy Mitchell have played a key role in new Texas grape industry. McPherson and Reed developed the first new commercial wine operation on the High Plains. As a chemistry professor, McPherson provided leadership in organizing the Llano Estacado winery, while Reed taught fruit culture at the university and directed the vineyard activities. However, Texas Tech's greatest contribution to the industry was Dr. Roy Mitchell of the chemistry department. Mitchell assisted growers throughout the state with enology problems and served as a positive support for all of the wineries. He also assisted the University of Texas Department of Lands staff with making and evaluating wines for their experimental vineyards. Mitchell has also played a key role in supporting the TGGA. He is currently assisting Dr. Bill

TABLE II. Texas Wineries

Winery	Location	Year	Gallons	Owner/Contact	Phone
Val Verde Winery	Del Rio	1883	10,000	Tommy Qualia	(512) 775-9714
Guadalupe Valley	New Braunfels	1975	10,000	Larry Lehr	(512) 629-2351
Llano Estacado	Lubbock	1976	200,000	Walter Haimann	(806) 745-2258
La Buena Vida	Springtown	1978	50,000	Bobby Smith	(817) 481-9463
Fall Creek	Tow	1979	65,000	Ed Auler	(512) 476-4477
Moyer Texas Champagne	Cedar Park	1980	25,000	Russell Smith	(512) 259-2000
Sanchez Creek	Weatherford	1981	6,000	Ron Wetherington	closed
Cypress Valley	Round Mountain	1982	23,000	Dale Bettis	closed
Château Montgolfier	Fort Worth	1982	5,000	Henry McDonald	closed
Wimberley Valley	Driftwood	1983	30,000	Dean Valentine	(512) 847-2592
Messina Hof	Bryan	1983	100,000	Paul Bonarrigo	(409) 778-9463
Pheasant Ridge	Lubbock	1983	45,000	William Gibson, Jr.	(806) 746-6033
Bell Mountain Vineyards	Fredericksburg	1984	50,000	Bob Oberhelman	(210) 685-3297
Ste. Genevieve/Cordier Estates	Fort Stockton	1984	1,500,000	Don Brady	(915) 395-2417
Schoppaul Hill	Ivanhoe	1984	20,000	John Anderson	closed
Sanuvas	Clint	1984	4,000	Jim Conway	closed
Bluebonnet Hill	Ballinger	1985	5,000	Antoine Albert	closed
Tejas	Mesquite	1985	8,000	Donald Frank	closed
La Escarbada XIT	Hereford	1986	9,000	Art Reinauer	closed

Preston Trail	Gunter	1986	10,000	Tom Greaves	(903) 433-1040
Slaughter/Leftwich	Austin	1986	30,000	Jane Leftwich Head	(512) 266-3331
St. Lawrence	Garden City	1987	35,000	Jerome Hoelscher	closed
Piney Woods	Orange	1987	3,000	Alfred Flies	(409) 883-5408
Cap✦Rock	Lubbock	1988	166,000	Kim McPherson	(806) 863-2704
Pedernales Valley	Fredericksburg	1988	12,000	Karl Koch	closed
Bieganowski Cellars	El Paso	1988	85,000	Victor Bieganowski	closed
Alamo Farms	Adkins	1988	4,000	Tom Pruski	closed
Sister Creek	Sisterdale	1988	4,000	Danny Hernandez	(210) 324-6704
Grape Creek	Stonewall	1989	15,000	Ned Simes	(210) 644-2710
Homestead	Ivanhoe	1989	10,000	Gabe Parker	(903) 583-4281
Hill Country Cellars	Cedar Park	1990	60,000	Fred Thomas	(512) 259-2000
Blum Street Cellars	San Antonio	1993		Tim Martin	(210) 222-2586
Hidden Springs	Pilot Point	1994	1,000	Jim and Lela Banks	(817) 665-8177
Delaney	Grapevine	1995	35,000	Jerry Delaney	(817) 355-1223
Becker Farms	Fredericksburg	1995	5,000	Richard Becker	(210) 644-2773

TABLE 3. Wine Production of the New Texas Grape Industry

Winery	County	1975	1976	1977	1978	1979
Val Verde	Val Verde	6,000	6,000	6,000	6,000	6,000
Guadalupe Valley	Comal	300	1,500	1,600	1,700	1,800
Llano Estacado	Lubbock		3,000	4,000	5,000	15,000
La Buena Vida	Parker				1,500	3,000
Fall Creek	Llano					600
Moyer Texas Champagne	Comal					
Sanchez Creek	Parker					
Cypress Valley	Blanco					
Château Montgolfier	Tarrant					
Wimberley Valley	Hays					
Messina Hof	Brazos					
Pheasant Ridge	Lubbock					
Oberhellmann	Gillespie					
Ste. Genevieve	Pecos					
Ivanhoe	Fannin					
Sanuvas	El Paso					
Bluebonnet Hill	Runnels					
Tejas	Dallas					
La Escarbada XIT	Deaf Smith					
Pedernales	Gillespie					
Preston Trail	Dallas					
Slaughter-Leftwich	Travis					
St. Lawrence	Glasscock					
Texas Winery Products	Lubbock					
Piney Woods	Orange					

One ton of grapes makes approximately 150 gallons of wine, or 63 cases, or 756 bottles. Texas vineyards yield from three to six tons per acre, on the average.

1980	1981	1982	1983	1984	1985	1986	1987
6,000	6,000	6,000	6,000	6,000	7,000	7,000	
1,200	600	1,600	500	2,000	2,000	2,000	1,500
14,000	15,000	13,000	47,000	35,000	47,000	96,000	112,000
3,500	7,000	10,000	15,000	17,000	11,000	3,000	11,000
1,000	3,000	5,000	8,000	13,000	10,000	20,000	32,000
5,000	5,000	5,000	5,000	5,000	5,000	4,800	12,000
	1,750	1,600	1,700	3,000	6,000	6,000	5,000
		3,000	7,000	15,000	23,000	17,000	31,000
		2,500	5,000	10,000	5,000	6,000	2,500
			14,000	35,000	21,000	20,000	20,000
			5,600	15,000	17,000	16,000	25,000
			3,200	7,000	9,100	11,000	20,000
				5,000	8,000	7,500	7,500
				182,000	275,000	400,000	155,000
				9,000	17,500	19,000	——
				4,200	4,200	——	——
					300	12,000	
					100	750	600
						1,600	3,800
						200	400
						500	
							4,000
							200

Lipe with enology research at Lubbock. He is also teaching a winemaking shortcourse through the Tech Department of Continuing Education.

University of Texas System: Bill Carr, formerly of The University of Texas System's University Lands-Surface Interests Office at Midland, was the first to recognize the potential for *vinifera* wine grapes in far West Texas in the early 1970s. He established experimental vineyards at Van Horn, Bakersfield, and Fort Stockton in 1975 and 1976. An experimental winery was started in 1978 to evaluate the wine potential of the grapes from the experimental vineyards. Dr. Charles O. McKinney headed the research in the experimental vineyards and winery. In 1981, The University of Texas System began planting a large commercial vineyard near Bakersfield, under the direction of E. E. "Gene" Drennan. This later became Ste. Genevieve Vineyards. Today, Steve Hartmann is the manager of The University of Texas System's University Lands-Surface Interests Office and manages the experimental vineyards and winery as well as oversees the lease of Ste. Genevieve Vineyards.

T. V. Munson Memorial Vineyard and Foundation: Dr. Roy Renfro has collected most of the Munson hybrid grape varieties from across the nation and has them growing in the T. V. Munson Memorial Vineyard at Grayson County College at Denison. All of Munson's works are being collected for permanent protection at the foundation. Continuing education courses in viticulture and enology are being taught at the college, and plans are under way for a new T. V. Munson Educational Center at the vineyard. Dr. Renfro has developed an outstanding two-year undergraduate program at the college.

SUMMARY

The Texas wine grape industry has made revolutionary growth in only ten years. However, it has not been without disappointment and failure. A high percentage of the vineyards planted never make it. All of these wineries meet with problems of one form or another. Because of this, potential growers should start small and grow slowly, one step at a time.

THE VITICULTURE AND ENOLOGY PROGRAM
AT GRAYSON COUNTY COLLEGE

Roy E. Renfro, Jr.
Administrator
T. V. Munson Viticulture and Enology Center
Denison, Texas 75020

The Viticulture and Enology Program at Grayson County College began in 1974, but the foundation for the program was laid in 1876, when Thomas Volney Munson arrived in Denison, Texas, to begin grape research which lasted his lifetime.

The Thomas Volney Munson Memorial Vineyard is on the campus of Grayson County College at Denison, an area Munson described upon arrival: "I have found my grape paradise!" He spent his life in the area developing superior grape varieties from the wild native grapes along the bluffs of the Red River and its tributaries.

After dedicated research during the 1970s, Wallace E. Dancy rediscovered Munson's achievements. Dancy's research led him to John Clift, state editor of the *Denison Herald* and author of the weekly newspaper column "The Wine Rack." These two collaborated and discovered that many of the Munson grape varieties still existed, mostly in private collections. Voluminous amounts of information were collected from many sources. As a result of the contacts made throughout the nation, an admiration society for T. V. Munson was launched. The W. B. Munson Foundation of Denison, Texas, was then contacted, and a project to honor T. V. Munson, brother of W. B., was initiated.

In the spring of 1974, a meeting held on the campus of Grayson County College was attended by Ben Munson III, foundation president; Truman Wester, president, Grayson County College; Ben McKinney, foundation director; John Clift, and Roy Renfro, Jr., seeking the expertise of the college's horticulture department in developing the memorial.

"I've asked the college to assist in this project," Munson said, "because I feel that this area has great potential for the grape industry. Grayson County College has the potential management skill, more so than any other institution in the area. I feel that we need this kind of expertise to make the project work." And so the T. V. Munson Memorial Vineyard was created.

The agriculture instructor for the college, Roy E. Renfro, Jr., was appointed administrator of the vineyard project and given the authority to proceed with the development of the memorial. When spring of 1975 arrived, the vineyard plot was ready to accept the first few grape varieties that had been located. From this meager beginning of five varieties, the memorial vineyard now has sixty-five of the Munson cultivars in production.

The T. V. Munson Memorial Vineyard is located on the West Campus of Grayson County College, one-half mile west of the intersection of State Highways 1417 and 691, between Sherman and Denison, Texas. The plan is to have as many as possible of the 300 Munson varieties in residence when the memorial is completed. The Munson three-wire "T" trellis system has been used with native cedar posts cut from timber along the banks of the Red River, where many of the native grapes Munson used are still thriving. A greenhouse has been constructed to aid in grapevine propagation. A turn-of-the-century-style brick maintenance building has been constructed adjacent to the greenhouse and serves as an area for propagation work and storage of the Munson grape cultivars. Permanent concrete walkways have been installed throughout the display vineyard to make tours more enjoyable.

Munson's contributions to world viticulture included a reclassification of the Vitis species; authoring the classic book *Foundations of American Grape Culture* in 1909; originating over 300 disease-resistant grape varieties specifically hybridized for the Southwest; and assisting the French government in finding the solution to the phylloxera epidemic which was devastating the French vineyards in the 1880s. The solution was Texas grapevine rootstocks, which were sent to France for grafting to *Vitis vinifera*. For Munson's assistance, the French bestowed upon him the title "Chevalier du Merite Agricole" in 1888.

On September 10, 1988, the T. V. Munson Viticulture and Enology Center was dedicated. It serves as a state and regional center for educational programs. The multipurpose structure, located on Grayson County College's West Campus, provides instruction to stimulate and encourage the art of grape growing and winemaking. The facility also serves as a repository for historical documents of international significance to the wine industry.

As an instructional site, the 5,000-square-foot facility houses a library for research documents and historical memorabilia; classroom and office space; and workroom facilities for processing grape plants, juice, and wine. Additionally, the center has classrooms for lectures, seminars, workshops, and demonstrations. Academic credit and credit-free courses, as well as meetings, will be conducted in the facility.

As a repository and research site, the center will house an extensive set of written materials related to the area of viticulture and enology. Among these documents are historical materials written about, and by, T. V. Munson regarding the breeding of grapes native to this area of the world.

In 1986–87, a grant was received by Grayson County College from the Texas Higher Education Coordinating Board to develop a viticulture and enology curriculum for the emerging Texas grape and wine industry. This was accomplished through the achievement of six objectives: validation of the current viticulture and enology curriculum; development of a new viticulture and enology curriculum with outcome competencies using the DACUM (Develop a Curriculum) Process; development of learning activities and evaluation measures; identification of learning activities and evaluation measures; identification of learning materials consistent with course syllabi for courses; and marketing of the newly developed curriculum.

The curriculum development process involved authorities from The University of Texas System; Texas A&M University; Texas Tech University; Texas Grape Growers Association; Texas wineries; University of California–Davis; California State University–Fresno; University of Arkansas; and Mississippi State University. The product of the curriculum development process was a two-year associate of science degree and an associate of applied science degree in viticulture and enology, which represents the most modern and innovative technical knowledge available today.

Grayson County College provides research and technical assistance with emphasis on service to commercial producers. Assistance projects include variety trials, fertility trials, grape plant and cutting distribution, credit and credit-free courses, seminars and workshops which are industry specific, and a tissue culture research project.

The future of the viticulture and enology program at the college will be measured by the quality of graduates and their success on the job. With the foundation laid by Munson and the Texas grape and wine industry, a bright future lies ahead if the program is monitored and improved as new technologies emerge.

An underlying philosophy of the program is to create constancy of purpose toward improvement of product and service. The aim is for graduates to be competitive, to stay in business, and to provide leadership for change.

A PROFILE OF THE TEXAS WINE
AND WINE GRAPE INDUSTRY

Texas Wine Marketing Research Institute
College of Human Sciences
Texas Tech University
P.O. Box 41162 / Lubbock, Texas 79409-1162
December 1994
Tim Dodd, Ph.D.
Marc Michaud
Véronique Bigotte
Denise Hood

EXECUTIVE SUMMARY

Economic Impact of the Texas Wine and Wine Grape Industry. The Texas wine and wine grape industry had an estimated total economic impact of $100 million on the Texas economy in 1993. Excise and sales tax revenue collected in 1993 on Texas produced wine resulted in an estimated total economic impact of $7.1 million on the Texas economy. Altogether, the Texas wine and wine grape industry directly and indirectly supported 2,149 Texas jobs and contributed an estimated $17.7 million to Texas paychecks in 1993.

Texas Wine Grape Production. Of the five Texas wine grape growing regions, the Texas High Plains region and the Trans-Pecos region each constituted 42 percent of total Texas wine grape producing acreage in 1993. The state's total acreage of commercial wine grapes stood at over 3,000 estimated acres in 1993 of which more than 2,600 acres were producing. The average price of a ton of Texas grapes returned to 1990 levels. Cabernet Franc, Cabernet Sauvignon, Chardonnay, and particularly Merlot commanded among the highest prices in 1993.

Texas Wine Production. Texas officially ranked 10th among U.S. wine producing states in 1993 following California, New York, Washington, Georgia, Oregon, Florida,

Ohio, New Jersey, and South Carolina. It may, however, be more appropriate to rank Texas as the nation's fifth largest wine producing state as several of the states listed do not possess sufficient vineyard acreage (*Vitis vinifera* or otherwise) to account for their wine production. Finally, fermenting and storage capacities of Texas wineries considerably exceeded actual production in 1993.

Texas Wine Consumption. Overall wine consumption trends in Texas have closely paralleled that of the United States from 1989 to 1993, with Table wines increasing in popularity more sharply in Texas compared to the rest of the nation. Wine Cooler consumption in Texas, although declining, remains an important part of the Texas wine market, with 13 percent of the market as compared to 7 percent nationally.

Texas remains the largest market for Texas wines, with approximately 97 percent of Texas produced wines being sold within the state in 1993. While supermarket wine sales continued to dominate overall Texas wine sales in 1993, Texas wine sales by retail outlet and industry structure highlights the traditional dependence of the state's largest wineries on supermarket and liquor store sales and the reliance of the state's smaller wineries on tasting room sales. Finally, the market share of Texas varietal and non-varietal wines in the state grew from 3.6 percent in 1992 to 5.9 percent in 1993.

Characteristics of Visitors to Texas Wineries/Texas Wine Trails. A study concerning the characteristics of visitors to Texas wineries was undertaken by the Texas Wine Marketing Research Institute in 1994. Visitors to Texas wineries have demographic traits closely related to those of wine consumers in general, such as higher incomes and higher levels of education than the general population. In terms of overall wine quality, 68 percent of visitors ranked California wines number one, 27 percent of visitors ranked Texas wines number one, and 52 percent ranked Texas wines number two. While only 25 percent of visitors had ever been to the winery they were visiting before the day they responded to the questionnaire, 42 percent planned their visit 24 hours before their tour and 46 percent planned their visit more than 24 hours ahead of time. Nearly 40 percent of visitors had purchased the wineries' products before, and nearly half of all purchases on the day of visitors' tours were made with the intention of consuming the wine within one week of the actual purchase.

Two major initiatives were conducted to help develop tourism by the Texas Wine Marketing Research Institute and the Texas Department of Agriculture. First, the Texas Department of Transportation erected a series of "point of interest" signs on public highways to guide visitors to Texas wineries in early 1994. Second, brochures for the Texas Hill Country and the Texas High Plains regions were created to further assist visitors in touring Texas wineries. The close proximity of the wineries within these two regions combined with the presence of a standardized highway winery signage program permitted the creation of "wine trails" with accompanying brochures.

ECONOMIC IMPACT OF THE TEXAS WINE AND WINE GRAPE INDUSTRY

Introduction. The economic impact analyses for 1991 and 1992 were prepared by Dr. Steve Morse and those for 1990, 1993, and projected for 1994 were prepared by Marc Michaud. These analyses use the Texas Input-Output Model, developed by the Economic Analysis Center of the Texas Comptroller of Public Accounts Office in Austin, Texas. Appropriate data used in these analyses were collected by the Texas Wine Marketing Research Institute, Texas Tech University.

Total Economic Impact. For 1993, the Texas wine and wine grape industry was responsible for an estimated total economic impact of nearly $100 million on the Texas economy. Of this $100 million impact, $34.9 million was direct impact (value of grapes and wine), and $65.2 million was indirect impact (generated by the re-spending multiplier effect). The estimated total economic impact of the Texas wine and wine grape industry has grown from a total of $91.2 million for 1990 to over a projected $121 million for 1994.

State Excise and Sales Tax Impact. The combined excise and sales tax revenue collected for 1993 on Texas produced wine resulted in an estimated total impact of nearly $7.1 million on the Texas economy. Of this $7.1 million total impact, $6.6 was generated by state and local sales taxes on Texas wines, and $0.4 million was generated by state excise taxes on Texas wines. The estimated total state excise and sales tax impact of Texas wines on the state's economy has grown from a total of $2.3 million for 1990 to over a projected $6 million for 1994.

Employment Impact. For 1993, the Texas wine and wine grape industry supported an estimated total of 2,149 jobs in the Texas economy. As a whole, the industry directly employed 664 Texans. Another 1,485 workers in Texas were employed indirectly through the generation of spending in other Texas industries. The estimated total employment impact of the Texas wine and wine grape industry has grown from a total of 2,032 jobs for 1990 to 2,600 for 1994.

Income Impact. For 1993, the Texas wine and wine grape industry was responsible for an estimated total income impact of $17.7 million on the state economy. Of this $17.7 million impact, $4.8 million was added directly to the wages and salaries of workers, and another $12.9 million was added to wages and salaries through the re-spending effect in other Texas industries. The estimated total income impact of the Texas wine and wine grape industry has grown from a total of $16.9 million for 1990 to over a projected $21 million for 1994.

Projections for 1994. Projections for 1994 are contingent upon the activity of the Texas wine and wine grape industry in 1994. At this time, the value of the 1994 wine grape crop is estimated at $4 million with wine production at approximately 1 million gallons and taxable withdrawals (i.e., sales) of over 900,000 gallons. The weighted average retail price for a bottle of Texas wine, however, may deviate from the $7.24 estimated for 1993 depending upon the responses of the state's wineries to the Institute's annual survey of the industry. Other data used in the analysis are considered stable and should not change the projections for 1994.

TEXAS VITICULTURAL AREAS (MAP 1)

Bell Mountain Viticultural Area. The Bell Mountain Viticultural Area, located in northeast Gillespie County about 15 miles north of Fredericksburg, was established in 1986. The appellation was the first in Texas and covers approximately five square miles on the southern and southwestern slopes of Bell Mountain. Further information on this appellation may be found in the *Federal Register*, dated October 10, 1986, Vol. 51, No. 197.

Fredericksburg in the Texas Hill Country Viticultural Area. The Fredericksburg in the Texas Hill Country Viticultural Area is located approximately 80 miles west of Austin, near the city of Fredericksburg in Gillespie County. The viticultural area consists of approximately 110 square miles. Further information on this appellation may be found in the *Federal Register*, dated December 22, 1988, Vol. 53, No. 246.

The Texas Hill Country Viticultural Area. The Texas Hill Country Viticultural Area was established in 1991. Covering a 15,000-square-mile area and fully or partially incorporating 22 counties, this region is the largest viticultural area in the United States. The Bell Mountain and Fredericksburg in the Texas Hill Country Viticultural Areas are located inside this appellation. Further information on this appellation may be found in the *Federal Register*, dated November 29, 1991, Vol. 56, No. 230.

Escondido Valley Viticultural Area. The Escondido Valley Viticultural Area was established in 1992. The appellation covers a 50-square-mile area along Interstate 10 between Fort Stockton and Bakersfield in Pecos County. Further information on this appellation may be found in the *Federal Register*, dated May 15, 1992, Vol. 57, No. 95.

Texas High Plains Viticultural Area. The Texas High Plains Viticultural Area covers a 12,000-square-mile area which includes much of the central and western Texas Panhandle region. Approved in January 1993, the Texas High Plains Viticultural Area fully or partially incorporates 24 counties. Further information on this appellation may be found in the *Federal Register*, dated March 2, 1993, Vol. 58, No. 39.

TEXAS WINE GRAPE PRODUCTION

Texas had over 3,000 estimated acres of wine grape vineyards in 1993, of which more than 2,600 acres were in production. Non-producing areas of wine grape vineyards numbered less than 400, and these were closely matched by new plantings over the past four years. Although new plantings seem to have increased in 1993, these are mostly in areas where unusually high prices have been seen for certain varieties and where particularly well managed vineyards have experienced some success in achieving desired yields.

Overall, prices per ton of wine grapes for the state have returned to 1990 levels. There were, however, significant differences between growing regions and notable changes over time. While Cabernet Franc, Cabernet Sauvignon, and Chardonnay prices have fluctuated since 1990, these varieties have consistently commanded some of the highest prices in the state. Merlot, in particular, has emerged as a popular variety with prices ranging from over $900 per ton to above $1,000 per ton.

Texas wine grape production value was estimated at $3.4 million in 1993, compared to $5.5 million in 1992. While most wine grape growing regions of Texas harvested moderate to good quantities of fruit, the Trans-Pecos produced only one-third of its normal levels due to a severe freeze in the spring of 1993. Production on the Texas High Plains, however, increased more than twofold as the region's vineyards recovered from the Halloween freeze of 1991.

With the exception of a few vineyards, Texas yields per producing acre remained unusually low compared to other winegrowing regions around the world. From the subjective responses of Texas wine grape growers, it would seem that growers often listed their weather damaged vineyards as producing acreage, thus resulting in the relatively low crop yields reported. It is worth noting, however, that despite the difficulties faced by Texas wine grape growers, the industry has grown to become a significant contributor to the state's agricultural diversity and remains an important part of the Texas economy.

TEXAS WINE PRODUCTION

Texas' 23 wineries indicated that they crushed over 4,300 tons of Texas grown wine grapes and produced 800,791 gallons of wine from the 1993 harvest. This is a substantial drop form 1992, when 26 wineries crushed 7,543 tons of Texas grown wine grapes and produced 1,475,346 gallons of wine. BATF figures indicate that 1,237,009 gallons of wine were produced for the 1992–1993 crop year.

Most of the drop in production was due to an unusually severe freeze in the spring of 1993 which hit the state's largest vineyards in the Trans-Pecos region. This freeze reduced the region's wine grape harvest to only 30 percent of the previous year's production. Due to one major spring freeze on the High Plains, a minor spring freeze in the Escondido Valley in 1994, and several minor freezes and hail thereafter, production will fall below the initial projections made by the state's wineries for 1994.

Texas ranked 10th among U.S. wine producing states in 1993 following California (1), New York (2), Washington (3), Georgia (4), Oregon (5), Florida (6), Ohio (7), New Jersey (8) and South Carolina (9). This is according to statistics compiled by the U.S. Department of the Treasury's Bureau of Alcohol, Tobacco and Firearms (BATF) for the 1993–1994 crop year, which covers wines removed from fermenters from July 1, 1993, to June 30, 1994. The reader is advised, however, that several large firms in some of the states listed produce a wide variety of products which do not necessarily originate from grapes produced in those states. Some of the states listed, for example, do not possess sufficient vineyard acreage (*Vitis vinifera* or otherwise) to account for their wine production. It may therefore be more appropriate to rank Texas as the nation's 5th largest wine producing state following California (1), New York (2), Washington (3), and Oregon (4).

The fermenting and storage capacities of Texas wineries have varied moderately from 1990 to 1993 over all production size categories. As compared to actual production over this same period, all size categories of Texas wineries appear to have considerable unused fermenting and storage capacities. This is especially true of the state's smallest wineries which have storage and fermenting capacities several times greater than their actual annual production.

Ten years ago small wineries (less than 10,000 gallons in annual production) produced one-half of all Texas wine. Today, the 12 smallest wineries which operate within the state produce about 4 percent of the wine produced in Texas. The four Texas wineries that produce 50,000 gallons or more grew from smaller beginnings or were established in the mid-1980s and today represent more than 75 percent of the state's total wine production. Finally, the state's remaining 7 wineries with production from 10,000 to 50,000 gallons per year are responsible for about 20 percent of Texas wine production.

Texas wineries are nearly 100 percent dependent on Texas-grown wine grapes, with little juice or bulk wine being brought into state (usually about of 1 or 2 percent of total annual production). On the other hand, significant amounts of juice, bulk or custom fermented wine, and especially wine grapes originating from within the state circulate in Texas among all levels of the industry. In fact, in a normal year, surprising amounts of juice and bulk wine originating from within the state actually leave Texas presumably to supply out of state vintners. In 1993, however, the unusually severe freeze mentioned earlier forced a much greater emphasis on fresh wine grapes with 41 percent purchased, 55 percent owned (with 1 percent juice and 3 percent bulk having been purchased) as there was little supplemental crop remaining to market outside of Texas.

Some Texas wineries producing over 50,000 gallons of wine seem especially dependent on outside sources of wine grapes. With less of a crop to work with in 1993 compared to the previous year, Texas wineries concentrated on producing varietal wines rather than non-varietal wines. Proportionally, the state's wineries produced 15 percent more varietal wine in 1993 than in 1992. Texas wineries that produced from 5,000 to 10,000 gallons of wine were the only exception to this trend and produced proportionally more non-varietal wine in 1993 than in the previous year.

In 1993, white wine composed 62 percent of Texas wine volume compared to 46 percent in 1992. However, red and blush Texas wines did not lose proportionally to their white counterparts across the four size categories of Texas wineries. While the former was true for the state's four largest wineries as a whole, wineries producing 10,001 to 50,000 gallons maintained approximately the same proportions of red, white, and blush wines as in 1992. Although the Texas wineries that produced up to 10,000 gallons made far less red wine, their production of blush wine increased noticeably in 1993.

Wet-Dry Status of Texas Counties (Table 17). Each individual precinct (the smallest possible geographical subdivision defined for voting purposes in the U.S.) potentially has different laws regarding the sale and commerce of alcoholic beverages. However, a general picture of Texas' wet-dry status is most easily illustrated at the county level. The number of counties in Texas in which distilled spirits are legal increased from 181 in 1990 to 184 in 1994. Combined with those five counties which specifically allow the sale of alcoholic beverages containing 14 percent or less alcohol by volume, 189 of the state's 254 counties allow sales of some form of wine. Eleven of the state's other counties only allow the sale of beer containing 4 percent or less alcohol by weight. Finally, the number of counties which are wholly dry decreased by three from 57 in 1990 to 54 in 1994.

Wine Consumption in Texas. Overall wine consumption in Texas has closely paralleled that of the United States from 1989 to 1993. An important national trend reflected in Texas is the increasing popularity of Table wines. This segment continues to grow at the expense of Dessert and Fortified wines, Champagne and Sparkling Wines, and Wine Coolers. The trend towards Table wines, however, is more pronounced in Texas compared to the nation as a whole.

Champagne and Sparkling Wine in Texas has closely followed a national decline in consumption with the exception of a modest increase in 1992. Wine Cooler consumption in Texas, although declining as well, remains a considerable component of the state's wine market. Compared to a national wine cooler market share of 7 percent and 5 percent in California and New York, wine coolers had 13 percent of the Texas wine market in 1993.

Texas Wine Sales. Proportionally, modest gains were made in out of state and international bottled wine sales in 1993. Texas, however, remains the major market for Texas wines as 97 percent of Texas bottled wine sales are made within the state. With regard to the form of these sales, 86 percent of Texas wine sales were in the form of bottled wine, 9 percent was sold as juice, and 5 percent was sold as bulk or custom fermented wine. With regard to the destination of these sales by form, 93 percent of juice sales and 41 percent of bulk or custom fermented wine sales were made out of state. Much of the sales in juice and bulk or custom fermented wine were juice sales made by wineries producing more than 10,000 gallons.

The largest retail outlet for Texas wines in 1993 was the supermarket. Of all the wine sold in Texas, 54 percent was sold in the state's supermarkets. Liquor and package stores represented the second largest retail outlet for Texas wines in 1993 at 21 percent, and another 14 percent of Texas wines were sold for on-premise consumption.

Winery tasting room sales represented 10 percent of Texas wine sales in 1993. Most of this volume was due to sales made by wineries producing more than 10,000 gallons annually. Wineries producing 10,000 to 50,000 gallons of wine annually matched their liquor store sales with their tasting room sales. Wineries producing more than 50,000 gallons, however, made four times as many sales through liquor stores as through their tasting rooms.

Compared to 1992, overall Texas wine sales proportionally shifted some 5 percent of sales from supermarkets to tasting rooms in 1993. This was generally the case for the largest and the smallest of Texas wineries. Those in the 5,000 to 10,000 gallon range, however, reduced their on-premise sales but increased both tasting room and liquor and package store sales. Wineries producing in the 10,001 to 50,000 gallon range significantly reduced their liquor and package store sales to the benefit of all remaining categories. Overall, however, the most significant feature of Texas wine sales by retail outlet and industry structure remains the traditional dependence of large wineries on supermarket and liquor store sales and the reliance of small wineries on tasting room sales.

Finally, the market share of Texas varietal and non-varietal wines in the state grew from 3.6 percent in 1992 to 5.9 percent in 1993. This figure is based upon taxable withdrawals of table wine from Texas wineries over shipments of all table wine in Texas. Although it excludes all other types of wines (Coolers, Champagne and Sparkling Wine, Dessert and Fortified wines, and Vermouth), it does include varietal and non-varietal wines available in packages over 1.5 liters.

CHARACTERISTICS OF VISITORS TO TEXAS WINERIES/TEXAS WINE TRAILS

Introduction. Sales of wine and winery souvenirs directly from the winery can be important for many wineries. Not only do tasting room sales provide wineries with an important retail outlet, they also give visitors the opportunity to learn about the wine industry and to taste wines with which they may be unfamiliar.

A study was undertaken during the summer of 1994 to determine the characteristics of people who visit Texas wineries. Six hundred eighty-four (684) consumers who visited Texas wineries during this period responded to the questionnaire. The following is a summary of the results obtained from that study. A more detailed report is available through the Texas Wine Marketing Research Institute.

Demographics. The average age of consumers was 40 years old. Seventy-seven percent of the respondents were 50 years of age. Visitors' incomes were high, with nearly two-thirds of respondents earning over $40,000 per year. Education levels were also above the national average. Sixty-six percent of visitors had a graduate or undergraduate degree.

Purchase Behavior, Previous Winery Visits, and Perceptions of Texas Wine. Most visitors to Texas wineries purchase wine from grocery stores (37%) and liquor stores (32%). Restaurants were also an important source of wine purchases (22%). Twenty-six percent of winery visitors had visited other Texas wineries before their visit on the day surveyed, although only 4 percent had visited 3 or more Texas wineries in the past.

In terms of overall wine quality, California wines were ranked number 1 by 68 percent of Texas winery visitors, and number 2 by 21 percent. Texas wines were ranked number 1 by 27 percent of Texas winery visitors and number 2 by 52 percent. New York, Washington, and Oregon wines were ranked 3, 4, and 5 respectively.

Twenty-five percent of visitors had been to the winery they were visiting before the day they responded to the questionnaire. Eleven percent had been to the winery two or more times before their visit on the date surveyed. Relatively few people decided to tour Texas wineries as they were just passing by. Most people planned to visit within the last 24 hours (42%) or decided to come to the winery longer than 24 hours (46%) before they made their tour.

Nearly 40 percent of visitors had purchased the wineries' products before their visit on the date surveyed. In addition, nearly half of all purchases were made for consumption within one week of actual purchases. To consume wine at a later time (31%) and to provide a gift for others (21%) were also important purposes of consumers making wine purchases.

Wine Trails. Early in 1994, the Texas Department of Transportation erected a series of "point of interest" signs on public highways to guide visitors to Texas wineries throughout the state. In coordination with the Texas Department of Agriculture and the Texas Wine Marketing Research Institute at Texas Tech University, brochures for the Texas Hill Country and the Texas High Plains regions were created to further assist visitors in touring Texas wineries. The close proximity of the wineries within these two regions combined with the presence of a standardized highway winery signage program permitted the creation of "wine trails" with accompanying brochures.

DIRECTORY OF TEXAS WINERIES

Bell Mountain/Oberhellmann Vineyards
Bob and Evelyn Oberhelman, Owners
HC 61, Box 22
Fredericksburg, Texas 78624
Ph.   (210) 685-3297
Fax   (210) 685-3657
Storage capacity: 30,000 gals.
Fermenting capacity: 19,000 gals.

Blue Mountain Vineyard
Ms. Nell Weisbach, President and Owner
Route 1, Box 7
Fort Davis, Texas 79734
Ph.   (915) 426-3763
Storage capacity: 3,500 gals.
Fermenting capacity: 3,500 gals.

Cap❖Rock Winery
Jim Stiles, Director of Operations
Route 6, Box 713K
Lubbock, Texas 79423
Ph.   (806) 863-2704
Fax   (806) 863-2712
Storage capacity: 134,000 gals.
Fermenting capacity: 118,000 gals.

Delaney Vineyards, Inc.
Jerry R. Delaney, President
1 Mile North of Lamesa on Hwy. 137
Lamesa, Texas 79331
Ph.   (806) 872-3177
Fax   (806) 872-8330
Storage capacity: 45,000 gals.
Fermenting capacity: 43,000 gals.

Fall Creek Vineyards
Ed and Susan Auler, Owners
1111 Guadalupe Street
Austin, Texas 78701   Winery
Ph.   (512) 476-4477   (915) 379-5361
Fax   (512) 476-6116   (915) 379-4741
Storage capacity: 65,000 gals.
Fermenting capacity: 55,000 gals.

Grape Creek Vineyards, Inc.
Ned and Nell Simes, Owners
P.O. Box 102
Stonewall, Texas 78671
Ph.   (210) 644-2710
Fax   (210) 644-2746
Storage capacity: 10,024 gals.
Fermenting capacity: 6,248 gals.

Guadalupe Valley Winery
Larry and Donna Lehr, Owners
1720 Hunter Road
New Braunfels, Texas 78130
Ph.   (210) 629-2351
Storage capacity: 9,500 gals.
Fermenting capacity: 6,700 gals.

Hill Country Cellars
Fred H. Thomas, Owner
1700 North Bell
Cedar Park, Texas 78613
Ph.   (512) 259-2000
Fax   (512) 259-2092
Storage capacity: 49,000 gals.
Fermenting capacity: 41,000 gals.

Homestead Winery
Gabe and Barbara Parker, Owners
P.O. Box 35
Ivanhoe, Texas 75447
Ph.   (903) 583-4281
Storage capacity: 11,305 gals.
Fermenting capacity: 8,945 gals.

La Buena Vida Vineyards
Steve Smith, Vineyard Mgr. and Winemaker
650 Vineyard Lane
Springtown, Texas 76082
Ph.   (817) 237-WINE
Storage capacity: 50,000 gals.
Fermenting capacity: 50,000 gals.

Llano Estacado Winery
Walter W. Haimann, President and COO
P.O. Box 3487
Lubbock, Texas 79452
Ph.   (806) 745-2258
Fax   (806) 748-1674
Storage capacity: 240,000 gals.
Fermenting capacity: 140,000 gals.

Messina Hof Wine Cellars
Paul and Merrill Bonarrigo, Owners
4545 Old Reliance Road
Bryan, Texas 77808
Ph.   (409) 778-9463
Fax   (409) 778-1729
Storage capacity: 110,000 gals.
Fermenting capacity: 85,000 gals.

Pheasant Ridge Winery
William E. Gipson, President
Route 3, Box 191
Lubbock, Texas 79401
Ph.   (806) 746-6033
Fax   (806) 746-6750
Storage capacity: 44,000 gals.
Fermenting capacity: 40,000 gals.

Piney Woods Country Wines
Alfred J. Flies, Owner
3408 Willow Drive
Orange, Texas 77630
Ph.   (409) 883-5408
Storage capacity: 3,000 gals.
Fermenting capacity: 1,000 gals.

Preston Trail Winery
Tom and Tiffany Greaves, Owners
Don and Ruby Prescott, Owners
Charles and Jimmie Britt, Owners
P.O. Box 275
Gunter, Texas 75058
Ph.   (903) 433-1040
Storage capacity: 11,696 gals.
Fermenting capacity: 10,116 gals.

Sister Creek Vineyards
Danny Hernandez, Vineyard Mgr. and Winemaker
Route 2, Box 2481C-1
Sisterdale, Texas 78006
Ph.   (210) 324-6704
Storage capacity: 4,500 gals.
Fermenting capacity: 3,500 gals.

Slaughter-Leftwich Vineyards
Scott Slaughter, President
107 RR 620S, Box 22F
Austin, Texas 78734
Ph.   (512) 266-3331
Fax   (512) 266-3180
Storage capacity: 40,000 gals.
Fermenting capacity: 32,000 gals.

Ste. Genevieve Wines (Cordier Estates, Inc.)
Leonard Garcia, President
P.O. Box 697
Ft. Stockton, Texas 79735
Ph.   (915) 395-2417
Fax   (915) 395-2431
Storage capacity: 1,200,000 gals.
Fermenting capacity: 1,200,000 gals.

Val Verde Winery
Tommy M. Qualia, Owner
100 Qualia Drive
Del Rio, Texas 78440
Ph.   (210) 775-9714
Storage capacity: 10,000 gals.
Fermenting capacity: 11,140 gals.

Note: Delaney Vineyards, Inc., is establishing a second facility in Grapevine. The Great Texas Champagne and Wine Company (winery) was being planned in Johnson City for the spring of 1995.

TEXAS WINERY DATA

BECKER VINEYARDS
Jenske Lane one mile off Highway 290
Stonewall, Texas
(210) 997-2948
Owners: Bunny and Richard Becker
Winemaker: Penny Adams
Bonded: 1995
Acreage: 36 acres grapes and 320 acres farm land—200
    planted in wildflowers
Tons produced: first crush in summer of 1995 with 3,000
    gallons anticipated of Chardonnay and Cabernet
    Sauvignon
Winery capacity: 10,000 gallons
Soil: Sandy loam
Hours open to public: 1996 opening
On-premise sales: Yes, in 1996

BELL MOUNTAIN VINEYARDS
HC 61, Box 22
Fredericksburg, Texas 78624
(210) 685-3297
Owner: Evelyn and Robert Oberhelman
Winemaker: Robert Oberhelman
Bonded: 1982
Acreage: 56
Tons produced: 72 in 1985
Estate grapes: 100%
1985 production: 10,500 gallons
1986 production: 10,500 gallons
Winery capacity: 20,000 gallons
Soil: Sandy loam with high iron and calcium oxides
Hours open to public: Saturday of March through Satur-
    day of December; Tour hours: 11:00 A.M., 1:00 P.M.,
    3:00 P.M. Saturdays. Other days by appointment.

CAP❖ROCK WINERY
Rt. 6, Box 713K
Lubbock, Texas 79423
(806) 863-2704
Tasting room and facility location: From South Loop 289
    travel south on U.S. Highway 87 for 5.7 miles and
    turn left (east) on Woodrow Road. Winery is on the
    right ½ mile off U.S. 87.
Visitor center open Monday–Saturday, 10:00 A.M.–5:00 P.M.
    and Sunday, 12:00 P.M.–5:00 P.M.
Current capacity: 139,000 gallons
Grapes: 119-acre estate vineyard, remainder contracted
    locally
Soil: Deep sandy loam
Owner: Plains Capital Corporation
President: De Pierce
Winemaker: Kim McPherson
Vice-president of Sales and Marketing: John Bratcher
Vineyard Manager: Mark Penna
Director of Operations: Jim Stiles

CORDIER ESTATES, INC.
STE. GENEVIEVE WINES
Headquarters: Ste. Genevieve Winery
Winery: 27 miles east of Fort Stockton
P.O. Box 697
Fort Stockton, Texas 79635
President/COO: Leonard Garcia
(915) 395-2417
FAX: (915) 395-2431
Winemaker: Don Brady
Bonded: 1987
Acreage: 1,000 acres
Tons produced: 3 to 7 per acre
Estate grapes: 100%
1988 production: 300,000 gallons (approximately)
1992 production: 1.1 million gallons
1993 production: a late frost initiated the need for a
    second pruning in June to force a second crop and
    late harvest for Chardonnay and Chenin Blanc. This

second pruning resulted in a high quality Chardonnay
and was the culmination of many trials and experiments which are conducted on a yearly basis. In 1994
there were more than eighty trials and experiments
being conducted in the vineyard.

1994 production: 900,000 gallons
Winery capacity: 1.5 million gallons
Soil: Limestone, silty clay loam

FALL CREEK VINEYARDS
P.O. Box 35
Tow, Texas 78672
915/379-5361
Vineyard manager: Tom Barkley
Office: 1111 Guadalupe Street
Austin, Texas 78701
512/476-4477
Owner: Susan and Ed Auler
Winemaker: Ed Auler
Director of Sales: Chad Auler
Bonded: 1979
Acreage: 65 acres, 75 planted by 1990
Estate grapes: 85%
Purchased grapes: 15%
1987 production: 12,000 cases
1988 production: 16,000 cases
1989 production: 20,000 cases
Winery capacity: 60,000 gallons
Hours open to the public: January–October, last Saturday
    of each month, 12:00–5:00 P.M.; other times by ap-
    pointment only
On-premise sales: Yes (on June 4, 1988, in a local option
    election, voters approved the sale of beer and wine)

GRAPE CREEK VINEYARDS
P.O. Box 102
Stonewall, Texas 78671
U.S. Highway 290 at South Grape Creek, 4 miles west of
    Stonewall
(210) 644-2710

FAX: (210) 644-2746
Owners: Ned and Nell Simes
Winemaker: Dr. Enrique Ferro
Bonded: 1989
Acreage: 17
Tons produced: 10 in 1994 (down from 35 in 1993 due to
    freeze)
1993 production: 5,200 gallons
1994 production: 5,800 gallons
Winery capacity: 11,000 gallons
Soil: Sand to clay
Hours open to public: Tasting Room — Tuesday-Saturday,
    10:00 A.M.–5:00 P.M. and Sunday, noon to 5:00 P.M.
On-premise sales: Yes
Wines: Fume Blanc, Cabernet Blanc, Chardonnay, Caber-
    net Sauvignon, and Cabernet Trois (Cabernet Franc,
    Ruby Cabernet, and Cabernet Sauvignon)

HILL COUNTRY CELLARS
1700 North Bell Blvd. (U.S. 183 North)
Cedar Park, Texas 78613
(512) 259-2000
FAX: (512) 259-2092
Owner: Fred H. Thomas
Winemaker: D. Russell Smith
Bonded: 1990
Acreage: 5
Estate grapes: 15%
Purchased grapes: 85%
1995 production: 45,000 gallons
Winery capacity: 60,000 gallons
Hours open to public: Tasting Room — noon–5:00 P.M. daily
Tours Friday/Saturday on the hour 1:00 P.M.–4:00 P.M. or
    Sunday by appointment

HOMESTEAD WINERY
P.O. Box 35
Ivanhoe, Texas 75447-0035
(903) 583-4281

Owners: Barbara and Gabe Parker
Winemaker: Mike Vorauer
Bonded: 1989
Capacity: 10,000 gallons
On-premise sales: No, but tours and special events are
    welcomed

LA BUENA VIDA VINEYARDS
(35 miles northwest of Fort Worth)
650 Vineyard Lane
Springtown, Texas 76082
(817) 220-4366
Tasting Room: 416 College Street / Grapevine, Texas
    76135 / (817) 481-9463
Owner: Bobby G. Smith
Winemaker: Steve Smith
Bonded: 1978
Acreage: 50, 12 under vines
Grapes: Chenin Blanc 55%, Cabernet 20%, Riesling 10%,
    Zinfandel 10%, Pinot Noir 5%
Winery capacity: 55,000 gallons
Soil: Sand and clay with gravel under base
Hours open to public: 7 days, Monday–Saturday, 11:00
    A.M.–5:00 P.M., Sunday, noon–5:00 P.M.
On-premise sales: Yes
Winery tours: By appointment

LLANO ESTACADO WINERY
3.5 miles east of U.S. 87
Lubbock, Texas 79452
(806) 745-2258
Owner: Llano Estacado Winery, Inc.
Winemaker: Gregory A. Bruni
Bonded: 1976
Acreage: 6
Tons produced: 5–8
Estate grapes: 5%
Purchased grapes: 95%
1993 production: 190,000 gallons (80,000 cases)
Winery capacity: 225,000 gallons

Soil: Deep sandy loam
Hours open to public: Monday–Saturday, 10:00 A.M.–5:00
    P.M.; Sunday, noon–5:00 P.M.; Gift shop, Tours, and
    Tasting
On-premise sales: Yes

MESSINA HOF WINE CELLARS
4545 Old Reliance Road
Bryan, Texas 77808
(409) 778-9463
Owner: Merrill and Paul Bonarrigo
Winemaker: Paul Bonarrigo
Bonded: 1983, planted 1977
Acreage: 40
Tons produced: 100 – 3 to 5 per acre
Estate grapes: 15%
Purchased grapes: 85%
1985 production: 18,000 gallons
1986 production: 25,000 gallons
1987 production: 21,000 gallons
1988 production: 21,000 gallons
1989 production: 25,000 gallons
1990 production: 42,000 gallons
1991 production: 52,000 gallons
1992 production: 60,000 gallons
1993 production: 72,000 gallons
1994 production: 87,500 gallons
1995 production: 112,000 gallons
Winery capacity: 120,000 gallons
Soil: Sandy and clay soils
Hours open to public: Monday–Friday 9:00 A.M.–5:30 P.M.;
    Saturday, 10:00 A.M.–5:00 P.M.; Sunday, noon–4:00 P.M.
On-premise sales: Yes

PHEASANT RIDGE WINERY
Rt. 3, Box 191
Lubbock, Texas 79401
(806) 746-6033
Owners: Texas Corporation
Winemakers: Enrique Ferro and Bill Blackmon

Bonded: 1982, vines planted 1979
Acreage: 48
Estate grapes: 80%
Purchased grapes: 20%
Production: 14,000 cases
Soil: Fine sandy loam, very calcareous, large lime content
Hours open to public: Tours welcome by appointment
On-premise sales: No

PINEY WOODS COUNTRY WINES
Orange, Texas 77630
(409) 886-1717
Owner: Alfred Flies
Bonded: 1987

PRESTON TRAIL WINERY
P.O. Box 275
Gunter, Texas 75058
(903) 433- 1040
Tom and Tiffany Greaves
239 Porter Road
Roanoke, TX 76262
(817) 430-4553
Owners: Tom and Tiffany Greaves and Don and Ruby
    Prescott
Winemaker: Tom Greaves
Bonded: July 7, 1986
Acreage: 19 acres
Tons produced: Sixth leaf, 2 tons per acre for each variety
    (Cabernet Sauvignon, Chardonnay, Chenin Blanc,
    Sauvignon Blanc, Semillon, French Colombard, Seyval
    Blanc)
Estate grapes: 100%
1986 production: 1,000 gallons
1987 production: 3,000 gallons
1989 production: projected amount is 10,000 gallons
Winery capacity: 10,000 gallons
Soil: Heavy clay
Hours open to public: Call for appointment
On-premise sales: No

SISTER CREEK WINERY
Route 2, Box 2481C-1
Sisterdale, Texas 78006
(210) 324-6704
Owner: Sister Creek Corporation
Winemaker and Vineyard Manager: Danny Hernandez
Bonded: 1988
Winery capacity: 4,500 gallons
Hours open to public: 7 days a week from noon to 5:00 P.M.
Acres: 5
Production: Proposed increase from 1,500 cases is sched-
    uled for 1996
Wines: Cabernet Sauvignon, Chardonnay, Pinot Noir, and
    a new wine introduced in 1995 by demand for a sweet
    wine, Muscat Canelli

SLAUGHTER-LEFTWICH VINEYARDS
4301 James Lane
Austin, Texas 78732
(512) 476-6708
Owners: June Leftwich Head, Scott Slaughter, Sally
    Slaughter, Lilly and Richard Leftwich Slaughter
Winemaker: Jim Johnson
Bonded: 1988
Acreage: 50 acres, planted 1979
Tons produced: 150 in 1986, 1987, 1988
Estate grapes: 100%
1988 production: 8,000 cases
1989 production: 10,000 cases
Winery capacity: 25,000 gallons
Hours open to public: Daily from May to October; Monday
    through Saturday, 10:00 A.M.–4:00 P.M.; Sunday,
    noon–4:00 P.M.

SPICEWOOD VINEYARDS
County Road 409
Spicewood, Texas 78669
Owners/Winemakers: Madeleine and Edward Manigold
Appellation: Texas Hill Country
Acreage: 10 under vines, expanding to 16 in 1996

Spacing: 5 x 10
Estate grapes: 100%
Winery capacity: 5,000 gallons
Soil: Sandy, clay, loam
Bonded: 1996
Hours open to the public: By appointment
Varietals: Merlot, Cabernet Sauvignon, Chardonnay,
    Sauvignon Blanc, Riesling, Zinfandel, Muscat, and
    Cabernet Franc

VAL VERDE WINERY
100 Qualia Drive
Del Rio, Texas 78840
(210) 775-9714
Owner: Thomas Qualia
Winemaker: Thomas Qualia; consultant, Dr. Enrique
    Ferro
Bonded: 1883
Acreage: 12
Tons produced: 10
Estate grapes: 50%
Purchased grapes: 50%
1994 production: 3,000 gallons
Winery capacity: 10,000 gallons fermenting; 14,000 gallons
    storage and aging
Soil: Sandy clay loam
Hours open to public: Monday–Saturday, 9:00 A.M.–5:00 P.M.
On-premise sales: Yes

TO YOUR HEALTH: A LITTLE WINE, IT TURNS OUT, IS GOOD FOR YOU

by Sarah Jane English

(Reprinted from *Food & Service* magazine, December 1987)

Early on, wine was the preferred beverage of conquerors, crusaders, fiefdom lords, and villagers. It was a matter of health, really, staying alive. Most water was at least mildly hazardous if not downright deadly, so the therapeutic properties of wine were discovered in a very meaningful way.

In those times, wine was not universally tantalizing. Members of royal families, naturally, had more wine than the poor. Nonetheless, much of it was muddy and sour, and spiced with foreign substances like honey or resin to make it more palatable. But wine enabled people to live long enough to grow fond of it and to praise and pass along its benefits.

The relationship between wine and health has substantial historical documentation, even though it wasn't understood. There are hundreds of stories concerning the laudable properties of wine. The doctors of Louis XIV recommended burgundy wine to enhance the monarch's longevity. Richelieu attributed his prowess in the boudoir to wine. A passage from the Talmud reads, "At the head of all sickness am I, blood: at the head of all medical remedies am I, wine. Only when no wine is available have recourse to drugs."

Today, moderate consumption of wine still plays a positive role in people's health and well-being. (Although if any type of alcohol is abused, of course, the opposite is true.) And research is bringing understanding to many mysteries about the ingestion of wine.

The Wine Institute, the trade association for more than 500 California wineries, has coordinated five symposia on wine and health. The February 1986 symposium, "Wine, Health and Society," brought together a distinguished panel of physicians and researchers who spoke on the healthful benefits of wine.

"We're in the midst of very profound changes in our lifestyle, and two themes underlie the change," says Kenneth Pelletier, an assistant clinical professor in the University of California School of Medicine's department of medicine and psychiatry. "One theme is informed choice, and a second concerns the involvement of individuals in policies that affect the changes."

Pelletier spoke about issues surrounding the moderate consumption of alcohol in our culture. He quoted statistics from a medical journal that gave an alarming trend and a hopeful solution: "Two-thirds of all U.S. deaths are premature, given our present medical knowledge, and about two-thirds of all years of life lost before age 65 are preventable." The solution lies in lifestyle choices.

"In the coming decades, the most important determinants of health and longevity will be the personal choices made by each person," said Pelletier. "A university report gives the four major preventable causes of premature death as tobacco, accidents, adolescent pregnancies, and alcohol; that is, generic alcohol, because there is no differentiation made.

"The report looks at alcohol as if all forms of it are equal, and there is absolutely no basis for that," he said. "Naturally, we're addressing the issue of moderate alcoholic beverage consumption in adults. Three major areas under study on moderate consumption are increased nutrient absorption, peak blood alcohol levels, and protective effects against disease."

Pelletier cited other studies. One reviewed countries with lower incidences of coronary heart disease as related to moderate consumption of wine. He noted that chemical mediators are one way in which moderate alcohol consumption may have a positive impact on health. Moderate consumption of wine decreases the tendency of blood platelets to stick together, which is a problem in heart disease. It also temporarily decreases blood pressure.

"I think the most significant variable here is that the

individuals engaged in moderate consumption will generally have a healthier lifestyle," he says.

Janet McDonald, a public affairs specialist with the U.S. Food and Drug Administration in San Francisco, spoke on "Wine and Nutrition" at the symposium. She revealed that wine contributes little to most normal daily nutritional requirements, but that it may make it easier for the body to absorb other nutrients. In a carefully controlled study of metabolism, moderate amounts of a red zinfandel wine taken with meals significantly enhanced the absorption of calcium, phosphorus, magnesium, and zinc. And another study found that iron added to white wine was more "available" to the body than iron added to red wine or a pure alcohol solution. And white wine had a far greater effect than the other beverages in increasing the absorption of iron from a mixed diet.

"These studies suggest that the non-alcoholic constituents of wine may be important," McDonald says.

"Are All Alcoholic Beverages Alike?" That was the title of the presentation at the symposium by David N. Whitten, a lecturer in physiology at the University of California at San Francisco. Whitten reported on a worldwide survey of scientific literature that highlighted differences among wine, beer, and distilled spirits in properties of alcohol absorption, metabolism, and human physiology.

Whitten's research showed that distilled spirits cause greater blood alcohol levels, even if they have been diluted to the same alcohol concentration as wine. Also, when equivalent amounts of the types of beverages are consumed, distilled spirits cause the greatest physiological and psychological impairment. Maximum blood alcohol levels are less for wine and distilled spirits consumed with or shortly after a meal. But, under those conditions, the blood alcohol level for wine is still less than that produced by distilled spirits.

"It is true that these beverages are similar in many ways," Whitten says. "All of them contain the same intoxicating ingredient. And it is true that the standard portions of each have about the same amount of alcohol in them. It depends on how much you pour into your system. To the person who is intent upon experiencing the effect of alcohol, these beverages are alike because it is possible to drink enough of them to become inebriated. From the perspective of the person who is an abusive drinker, they have the same effect. But on the other side, there are many, many ways in which the beverages are different."

Whitten pointed out some of the differences. For instance, wine is used for many social, behavioral, religious, and ritualistic purposes.

"Wine enjoys a special place in sacraments observed in the Jewish faith and in many Christian denominations," he says. "It is used in family rituals, it is used in wine-tasting courses, and many universities offer wine appreciation courses. In these ways, then, it is clear that wine is a different beverage.

"Studies have shown repeatedly that the peak blood level of alcohol is greater by far after drinking hard spirits than after drinking wine, even when the same amount of alcohol is consumed or when the beverages are consumed with or after a meal," Whitten says. "It seems clear to me that these beverages are not the same."

Whitten believes it is important to note additional study results.

"In the first 15 to 30 minutes after drinking alcoholic beverages, for hard spirits, the blood level of alcohol to which the brain is exposed may be as much as 2.5 times greater than that for wine," he says. "Studies also show that if you insist on eating and drinking to excess, it does not matter how much you eat, and it does not matter what you're drinking, you'll end up drunk."

The American Heart Association has revised its guidelines for heart-healthy eating. For the first time, the directives include recommendations for alcoholic beverages, according to Connie Root-Bardin, a licensed dietitian who is a spokesperson for the American Heart Association. The new guidelines suggest that daily consumption of alcohol should not exceed 50 milliliters (about 1.5 ounces), the amount found in two glasses of wine.

"The link between cardiovascular disease and alcohol is

still being studied," Root-Bardin says. "But drinking has increased dramatically in the last 30 years, with alcohol accounting for five percent of all the calories Americans consume, so we needed to address the issue. There appears to be a relationship between alcoholic beverage consumption and high blood pressure in susceptible people, especially if they consume more than four drinks a day. Modest consumption, however, can be beneficial."

On May 4, 1987, the cultural and health values of wine in American life were examined at a seminar on "Wine, Culture and Healthy Lifestyles" presented at the New York Academy of Sciences by the Winegrowers of California. Also, Carol and Malcolm McConnell discussed their book *The Mediterranean Diet.* According to the McConnells, the diet of Mediterranean villagers is built around a trio of staples—grain, olives and grapes—and is supplemented with fresh fruits and vegetables, fish, garlic, and onions. For example, the typical lunch and dinner of Greek peasants emphasizes bread or pasta and vegetables prepared with olive oil.

"This diet is low in milk and butter, meat, refined sugar and flour," say the McConnels. "The grape portion of the dietary triad takes form predominantly as wine served with meals. An average of two glasses of wine per day is drunk with meals. The secret of healthful nutrition is as old as the Bible. Doctors have found startling evidence that the combination of foods in the traditional diet of Greek and Italian village cultures helps shield them from the ravages of heart disease and many forms of cancer."

The clear association of wine with food is the most important factor in helping wine slip easily into the "fitness generation," writes Jane Brody, science writer and personal health columnist for the *New York Times.* She adds that wine also has the ability to relax the drinker and is one reason some hospital patients are now being offered wine with their meals. Research into the topic produced a surprising theory: The main relaxing agent in the wine may not be alcohol.

"While wine's ability to mellow (relax the person drinking it) has long been attributed to its alcohol content, an interesting study among laboratory rats at Rutgers University suggests that wine's alcohol-free portion is the primary tranquilizer," Brody says. "The animals were given water, wine, and alcohol-free wine residue. Then they were tested for their activity level and sensitivity to shock. Water produced no change, while wine as well as the wine residue reduced their activity levels and sensitivity to mild electrical shock. There may be something really special about wine."

A number of groups and events are devoted to educating the public on matters of wine and food. The American Institute of Wine and Food, for example, is a nonprofit, educational organization founded in 1981 to advance the understanding, appreciation and quality of wine and food. Its collection of data and literature are excellent sources on various aspects of wine and food, and its Conference on Gastronomy presents important information annually. At the 1986 conference in Dallas, a panel addressed the issue of additives in American wines.

One such additive is sulfites. According to Hugh Johnson, author and wine authority, sulfur dioxide has been used since Roman times to sterilize wine barrels. Pasteur also used it as a sterilizing agent. Then it was found that sulfur dioxide inhibited the oxidation of wine, so the chemical became important in wine production. The ecology of the vineyard is important too. Fertilizers often contain sulfur. Also, yeasts produce sulfur, which keeps wines biologically stable.

However, many persons are allergic to sulfites and have demanded labeling laws to inform them of its use. The trend in California is to use less sulfur dioxide in winemaking, but because it is a natural outcome of wine production, anyone allergic to sulfites should not drink wine.

Research by the National Cancer Institute and the Harvard Medical School, as reported in *Newsweek* and *Time* in May 1987, found a relationship between alcohol and breast cancer. The research found that for women who drink even moderate amounts of alcohol, the risk of developing breast cancer is 30 to 50 percent greater than for women who do not drink alcohol. But the Harvard study revealed something about wine that the press largely overlooked: "The risk of breast cancer associated with alcohol intake from beer and liquor remained significantly elevated, but the association with wine was reduced and not significantly different from that in nondrinkers."

According to *Time*, "Confronted with demands for specific advice on drinking behavior in light of the new findings, doctors began hedging. Said Peter Greenwald, director of NCI's cancer-prevention-and-control division: 'We don't have the information to be making a public recommendation at this point.' One problem is that these early studies simply associate drinking with cancer; they do not show a cause-and-effect relationship or offer an explanation of the mechanisms involved.

" 'Even if there is such a relationship, it may be far from direct,' said Robert Hiatt of the Kaiser Permanent Medical Care Program in Oakland, who reported an alcohol-breast cancer link in 1984: 'So far, this is an epidemiological finding that has been repeated, leading to concern. As yet, there is no linkup with biology.'

"Nonetheless, a consensus exists that women who are already at risk for breast cancer (those with high-fat diets, who are over fifty, or have a family history of the disease) should probably drink less."

Aristotle advocated moderation in most things, a lesson mortals seem bound to defy. Nonetheless, Americans are becoming increasingly aware of favorable diets, nutrition, and healthy practices. Part of their program is discovering the pleasurable — and healthful — benefits of moderate amounts of wine.

Index